John Dawes's
BOOK OF
WATER GARDENS

John Dawes

Distributed in the UNITED STATES by T.F.H. Publications, Inc., One T.F.H. Plaza, Neptune City, NJ 07753; in CANADA to the Pet Trade by H & L Pet Supplies Inc., 27 Kingston Crescent, Kitchener, Ontario N2B 2T6; Rolf C. Hagen Ltd., 3225 Sartelon Street, Montreal 382 Quebec; in CANADA to the Book Trade by Macmillan of Canada (A Division of Canada Publishing Corporation), 164 Commander Boulevard, Agincourt, Ontario M1S 3C7; in ENGLAND by T.F.H. Publications Limited, Cliveden House/Priors Way/Bray, Maidenhead, Berkshire SL6 2HP, England; in AUSTRALIA AND THE SOUTH PACIFIC by T.F.H. (Australia) Pty. Ltd., Box 149, Brookvale 2100 N.S.W., Australia; in NEW ZEALAND by Ross Haines & Son, Ltd., 18 Monmouth Street, Grey Lynn, Auckland 2, New Zealand; in the PHILIPPINES by Bio-Research, 5 Lippay Street, San Lorenzo Village, Makati Rizal; in SOUTH AFRICA by Multipet Pty. Ltd., 30 Turners Avenue, Durban 4001. Published by T.F.H. Publications, Inc. Manufactured in the United States of America by T.F.H. Publications, Inc.

CONTENTS

John Dawes

About the Author

John Dawes became involved in aquatics at the age of seven when he started keeping Mosquito Fish in a small battery tank and was captivated by their fascinating, if cannibalistic, breeding habits. That early experience triggered off an all-embracing interest in aquatics that resulted, some years ago, in the fulfillment of one of his burning childhood ambitions: editorship of the UK aquatic magazine *Aquarist & Pondkeeper*.

After a period of eight years as a schoolteacher, plus another eight as a Lecturer in Education at the University of Bath in Avon, England, John embarked on a full-time freelance career that takes him far and wide on consultancy, judging, lecturing and writing assignments.

A graduate of the University of Keele, and a Chartered Biologist, John has other academic qualifications as well, including Membership of the Institute of Biology and Fellowship of both the Zoological and Linnaean Societies of London.

In addition to his educational appointments, John has been Senior Consultant to a major fish food manufacturing company and is currently Aquatic Correspondent to Pet Business World, Scientific Adviser (Aquatics) to the International Pet Trade Organisation, Contributing Editor to various journals, and has recently been appointed member of the Freshwater Fish Specialist Group of the Species Survival Commission of the International Union for Conservation of Nature and Natural Resources.

John has written over 500 publications for educational, scientific and popular journals, as well as several books on aquaria, ponds and general fishkeeping. He is also President of several specialist societies in the UK and travels on regular expeditions to expand his knowledge of aquatic plants and animals in the wild.

His other interests include a passion for Asian cookery and Mediterranean wildflowers.

John, who was born in Gibraltar in 1945, and his wife live near Bath in England, and near Manilva in southern Spain.

INTRODUCTION

Pondkeeping is growing in popularity year by year. This upsurge in interest is, quite naturally, accompanied by a similar one in the range of ponds, equipment, accessories, ornaments, fish and plants for sale. So much so, that, to the uninitiated, the whole subject of ponds and their maintenance can appear exceedingly complex and confusing.

This couldn't be further from the truth. Building or installing a pond and maintaining it successfully can be a relaxing, rewarding, spectacular, easy, and worthwhile activity. One can, of course, spend a small fortune on setting up a pond. But equally superb, well balanced arrangements can be comfortably created for quite a modest outlay.

I have tried in this book to present the subject in an easy-to-follow manner in the hope that this will help existing and potential pond owners to make rational decisions tailored to their own personal circumstances and needs.

Step-by-step guides to construction, stocking and maintenance form essential components of the text, but, wherever possible, I have also dealt with the principles behind these directions. It is my belief that this approach leads to a more complete appreciation and relatively trouble-free, full enjoyment of the art of pondkeeping.

One emphasis that runs through the book is the pond owner's responsibility to consider and respect the needs of fish, plants and other inhabitants. Their lives are in our hands and we must neither ignore this fact nor let our personal whims interfere with the well-being of the animals and plants in our care. If you are new to pondkeeping, welcome to a great hobby. If you are an established pondkeeper, I wish you continued success and enjoyment.

John Dawes

The difference between a 'pond' and a 'pool' is often not clearly defined. The above photo is of an informal garden pond as opposed to a natural pool. The pond was created by man with the specific intention of practicing the garden pond hobby.

1
Setting the Scene

When we talk of a body of water containing fish or plants, or both, established in a patio or garden, usually for recreational purposes, we refer to it as a pond. Yet, if we look at the available literature, both books and magazines, we find two words in general use. 'Pool' and 'pond' can repeatedly appear on the same page, in the same paragraph or even in the same sentence, often used interchangeably to refer to the same body of water.

So what do we have in our gardens and patios - pools or ponds? My dictionary defines them as follows:

Pool. A small body of still water; a temporary or casual collection of water or other liquid; a puddle; a deep part of a stream.

Pond. A small, usually artificial, lake; the stretch of water between locks in a canal.

Clearly, a pool and a pond have a number of features in common. But a pool needs to be small and still, temporary or part of a stream.

A pond does not have to fulfill such criteria (after all, even a small lake can be relatively big.) This, added to 'usually artificial,' tips the balance firmly in favor of a pond.

Ponds are usually artificial and they are usually small lakes. They can also vary greatly in design, shape, construction and content and can incorporate moving water in a variety of forms, including fountains, waterfalls and watercourses. All these variables can be accommodated comfortably under the term **'pond'** as defined by my dictionary. (The second pond definition referring to locks in canals, does not, of course, invalidate the first definition.)

Below is an expanse of water that qualifies as a pool because it is a small (the term is relative) body of still water formed, in this case, in a deep and broad part of an existing stream.

NATURAL VS. FORMAL PONDS

A further possible source of confusion arises from the use of the terms **'natural'** and **'formal'** describing types of ponds. The fact is that very few people are fortunate enough to have a genuinely natural pond in their garden. What is more, the number of natural ponds found in the wild has steadily decreased over the years— silent victims of the bulldozer, drainage schemes and many other 'progress-associated' programs.

To qualify as a true natural pond, a body of water must be formed of natural products, without human intervention, and must be inhabited by wild plants, fish, amphibians, invertebrates and other organisms. We only begin to appreciate the real significance of the term 'natural' if we apply these criteria to the vast majority of ponds.

When garden and patio ponds are referred to as 'natural,' it is their shape more than any other single feature that is usually taken into

Pictured below is a formal pond in the Japanese style. While it does not have straight edges or marble fountains, it has the symmetry and design.

consideration. What we mean by natural, then, is a pond with an irregular, informal shape, as opposed to a formal one with straight sides, matching inlets, smooth and regular curves. A natural shape can be achieved in many ways. Even concrete can be worked into informal designs. However, the two most popular approaches adopted in obtaining a natural outline involve the use of either prefabricated ponds or pond liners.

Each of these will be dealt with in greater detail later. I only want to make two points here:
1. Liners provide maximum flexibility and so are better suited to the natural approach than most other materials.
2. Considering how inaccurate the word natural is when applied as I have described, perhaps we should avoid using it and restrict ourselves to the term 'informal'.

We could perhaps use the term 'natural' for ponds stocked with plants and animals belonging entirely to native species. But, even here, the term 'wildlife pond' seems more appropriate.

THE INFORMAL POND

Irrespective of the material used in their construction, all informal ponds have one feature in common—a lack of symmetry. They are therefore characterized by an absence of straight edges or smooth, matching curves. To be truly informal, one would have to choose a random shape. But this is considerably more difficult than it sounds. Just try drawing a random shape and you will see what I mean. Even if you can produce a genuinely random outline, it will not necessarily be attractive, or even appropriate. In the end, most people compromise. So long as a shape is assymmetrical, pleasant to look at, and adequately provides for its aquatic inhabitants, it can be regarded as informal.

Informal ponds tend, on the whole, to be stocked with a wide variety of plants and fish and are often landscaped into the surrounding area so that they form an integral part of a larger whole. The arrangement of the plants is dictated by the position of the shelves which are themselves determined by the overall shape of the pond.

Putting all the above together, and adding a little creative flair, it is easy to see how a good

This large informal pond has been made exceedingly attractive with just a few basic additions: the incorporation of an unobtrusive footbridge, the addition of a small island, and the maintenance of the wildlife surrounding the pond.

informal design can develop into a feature of outstanding beauty and charm.

THE FORMAL POND

At the other end of the spectrum are **formal** ponds, magnificent examples of which can be found in the grounds of stately homes and palaces. In some of these, their symmetry takes priority over everything else. In fact, some formal ponds contain no fish at all. Their beauty lies in their shape, or the design and use made of lighting or moving water in the form of watercourses, fountains and other features. Although they are as far removed from the concept of the natural pond as possible, they are just as 'valid.' They merely have different qualities.

All these qualities can be incorporated quite easily and effectively into the design of a patio or garden pond. Other desirable features, such as ease of maintenance, can also be worked into the basic plan of any small formal set-up. In

contrast to informal designs, formal ones are characterized by straight edges, smooth, matching curves and other features never found under natural conditions. The range of fish and plants is often more restricted than in informal ponds.

Formal systems tend to have regularly spaced, shaped and sized planting shelves designed to produce an overall pattern. Fountains and other ornaments also occur more frequently in formal arrangements. While natural/informal pondkeepers may frown on the designs chosen by their formal counterparts, there is no denying that a well planted formal pond, particularly if incorporated into a similarly laid out patio or garden setting, can look impressive, elegant and very pleasing to the eye.

SOME OTHER POSSIBILITIES

Some gardens or patios may be too small, or just not suitable, for a pond. Or one may want a modest-sized decorative feature, rather than a fully fledged system. Several options are available for either situation, each with its own characteristics and attractions.

Virtually any non-toxic container can be converted into a small water feature. Some that

This formal pond combines both straight and curved edges; it also makes use of a stone fountain which adds to the attractiveness of the pond.

have been used with considerable success are ceramic bathtubs, refrigerator liners or sinks, and half-barrels or water butts, often referred to as tub ponds.

Millstones have also been developed into moving water features by means of a few simple, ingenious adaptations, including the installation of a water/fountain pump. These millstone fountains have all the soothing effects of moving water, housed in a compact unit which can be installed to stunning effect in the smallest of patios. Details of small water systems will be discussed in greater detail later in this book.

I have mentioned them here just to present a fuller picture of the range of options open to anyone wishing to include water as part of a patio or garden layout. Though I have divided these into informal ponds, formal ponds and small water features, the briefest consideration will show that the number of possibilities is actually endless and that the dividing lines between the categories are nicely fuzzy. That, in my opinion, is the way it should be. We are, after all, dealing with an infinitely variable, flexible, exciting spectrum which can be tailored to meet the requirements of every potential pondkeeper, as well as all the plants and animals that can be accommodated in ponds.

MAIN CHARACTERISTICS OF VARIOUS SYSTEMS

Type of System	Main Characteristics
Informal Pond	Irregular shape (lack of obvious symmetry.) Relatively wide selection of plants and/or fish.
Wildlife Pond	Irregular shape. Selection of plants and/or fish—restricted to native species. All forms of natural waterlife encouraged, e.g. frogs, toads, newts, dragonflies, etc.
Formal Pond	'Artificial' shape. Symmetrical/matching sides common. Even if patterns are not repeated, the pond outline shows obvious signs of planning. Range of plants and/or fish usually more restricted than in informal set-ups. Ornaments, fountains, etc., are common features.
Tub/Sink Pond	Small water feature with restricted stocks of plants and/or fish. Ideally suited for small areas. Free-standing and compact.
Millstone Water Feature/Pebble Fountains	Emphasis on appearance, particularly water movement. No fish and/or plants. Ideal for patios.

THE ESSENTIAL CONSIDERATIONS

Among the earliest decisions a prospective pond owner has to make (certainly before *anything* is bought) is how to make the best use of the space available. Top of the list must be a genuine regard for the needs of the plants and animals seen in the mind's eye as forming the ideal combination. Fantasy and reality must be brought as close together as possible. Failure to do so will invariably result in inappropriate decisions with inevitable, distressing consequences. We must always remember that plants and pond animals cannot complain. They just die if conditions are seriously out-of-step with their requirements.

Having decided to have a pond or other water system of whatever kind, two alternative approaches are possible.

One of the best aspects of the garden pond hobby is the multitude of possibilities allowed in the shaping and decorating of the pond. As is demonstrated by the many water features above, one can add a truly personal touch to one's garden pond.

SETTING THE SCENE

One can start from the human standpoint by saying, 'I am going to have a pond measuring x meters in length, x meters in width and x centimeters in depth, and I am going to stock it with 200 large fish of different colors...'

The alternative approach views the matter from the plants' and animals' point of view, as well as the human, and goes something like this: 'I would like to keep a number of varieties of Goldfish in attractive surroundings which should include colorful Water Lilies and marginal plants. What sort of pond would meet the plants' and fishes' requirements as well as my own?'

If the first approach is taken, there is likely to be a marked mismatch between what the pond owner wants and what the pond inhabitants need. This mismatch will make its presence felt sooner or later (usually sooner.) The problems can be ironed out in time and once they are, one usually ends up with a pond that suits the owner and the inhabitants, though considerable hardship and distress will have been experienced on the way. Of course, the other possibility is that the whole project will be given up as a bad idea after a brief, unhappy relationship.

Much of this can be avoided by following the second approach outlined above. It is not foolproof, but the mismatch is likely to be minimal, the experience enjoyable and the relationship long-lasting. It is possible to have an attractive pond well suited to all parties concerned. All it requires is that most valuable of human qualities—common sense!

This applies as much to new ponds as to those inherited when one moves to a new property. With the latter, one should note what stocks the inherited pond holds, ask the necessary questions about the suitability of the existing conditions for the inhabitants, and oneself, and then alter things accordingly if necessary.

But there is such a wide range of possible arrangements that making fundamental decisions are often difficult.

The fantasy/reality relationship mentioned earlier plays a very important role here too. You

Anyone can have a garden pond. If you are limited by space or finances, a tub, sink, clay pot, or other pond medium may be the solution. Ponds can beautify whatever area you own or inhabit so don't feel limited.

Consider your finished product permanent. Therefore, realize your goal and intention before proceeding with purchase and construction.

may want a wildlife pond, but if your garden is set out in a formal fashion, it would look totally out of place. If so, you must reassess your priorities.

The ideal decision, from the pond's point of view, would be to reorganize the garden, converting it completely into a wildlife garden, or at least, one in which a section can be allocated to wildlife.

Though deciding about the type of pond may prove difficult, it must not be rushed. Remember that mistakes made at this early stage can prove difficult and expensive to rectify later. Early considerations must not only concern the type of pond—formal, informal or wildlife—but also the type of construction material. These can be grouped into several categories:

- Concrete, cement, brick, blocks.
- Liners, e.g., polyethylene, PVC, butyl.
- Prefabricated materials, e.g., plastic, fiberglass.
- Wood, as in tub ponds.
- Ceramic, as in sink ponds.
- Artificial/reconstituted/natural stone, as in millstone water systems.

Each of these materials has a number of advantages and disadvantages. Personal circumstances and opinions will influence the final decision one way or another.

Housing a durable liner in a concrete and block construction is an effective way of creating a pond that will provide a lifetime of beauty and enjoyment.

CONCRETE, CEMENT, BRICKS AND BLOCKS

Concrete, overlaid with cement, is an extremely durable combination, and a pond constructed of these materials can be made to fit any shape. Such flexibility is an important advantage. If brick and/or blocks are worked into the plans, then a vast range of raised, formal designs becomes possible. On the debit side, concrete is not the easiest of materials to work with, particularly during hot, dry periods. Consequently, the best time of year for constructing a concrete or cement pond is autumn, when the air is relatively humid but frosts have not yet started,

If concrete cracks, it can prove difficult to repair. It is often a major operation to repair quite a small fracture, particularly if this occurs below water level.

Another potential drawback is the fact that the lime which concrete and cement release is highly toxic to plants and animals. Waterproofing, sealing, or a long maturation period, accompanied by repeated filling, draining, and refilling, are therefore essential to make concrete ponds safe.

LINERS

Butyl liners are not only durable but also tremendously flexible and quite easy to work with. What is more, butyl-lined ponds can be installed virtually all the year 'round.

Despite these and other advantages, it would be wrong to think of butyl as the ideal solution for every occasion. For example, it is next to impossible to achieve clean-cut straight lines, or perfect unwrinkled curves. This could present problems if a trim, precise, formal layout is desired.

Butyl is also expensive and this aspect of pond construction can be an important deciding factor. If a temporary pond is required, it might make more sense to use a cheaper, though less flexible or less durable, liner.

Polyethylene, PVC (polyvinyl chloride) and PVC laminated with nylon or terylene weave are, in ascending order of price, the most popular alternatives to butyl. Polyethylene is the least durable of these liners. It is also sensitive to ultraviolet radiation (a component of sunlight), becoming brittle over a period of time. However, it is inexpensive and therefore a good choice for temporary ponds.

PVC, especially if reinforced, is considerably more durable than polyethylene. It is also more expensive, though still cheaper than butyl.

PREFABRICATED MATERIALS

The two materials commonly used in prefabricated ponds are plastic and fiberglass. In recent years, black polyester ponds have also appeared.

Of the three, plastic is the weakest. Fiberglass, particularly if reinforced, and black polyester, are considerably stronger and can last for many years. In fact, some companies dealing in these ponds offer guarantees of 10 years or even longer.

For the pond owner who does not wish to plan the shape of a pond, or build it afterwards, a prefabricated system presents a very welcome way out. There are shapes and sizes to meet most needs, though some designs are rather shallow. This can present considerable problems with the survival of some pond inhabitants in areas that experience harsh winters.

Many prefabricated ponds are also on the small side. Though this could be seen as an obvious disadvantage where large, permanent collections are envisaged, it can prove a significant advantage for temporary, quarantine, or hospital quarters. Small ponds of this type can also provide excellent, manageable facilities for rearing young fish during spring and summer.

Children love these ponds too because they are so accessible, and parents like them because they are safe. If frogs, toads and newts are seen as welcome additions to a water garden, small prefabricated ponds can provide ideal spawning sites, particularly if fish are omitted during the appropriate months of the year.

Children love ponds. They are fascinated by the plants and wildlife within them. A wonderful way to educate children to the ways and means of the environment is to provide them with access to a garden pond—supervised access, of course.

An advantage of lined ponds over prefabricated ones is the flexibility of the lined pond. Lined ponds can be set in almost any shape you desire, always keeping foremost in mind the needs of the various inhabitants. Pictured below is an informal lined pond.

To aid you in designing your pond, we have included several possible pond designs. Pictured below is what is commonly called the canyon construction.

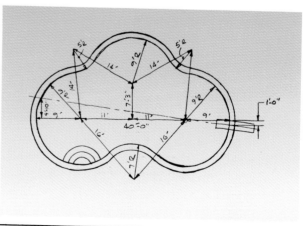

Above: If the soil permits it may well be possible to use   earth and minor construction to help create a more 'natural-looking' construction. **Below:** Appearing in various locations throughout this book are line drawings of potential pond designs. They are based on 40' ponds.

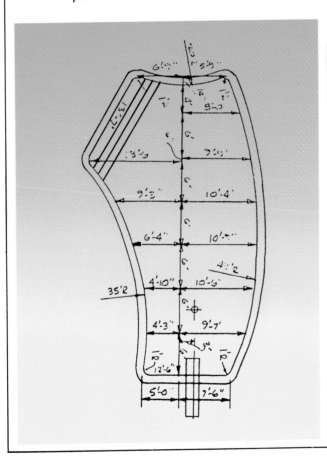

WOOD

Wood has already been mentioned in connection with tub ponds, but it can also be used to construct raised, formal ponds. Tub ponds consist of barrels cut in half, so they are usually watertight. It is possible, therefore, for anyone to create a very attractive water feature in less than half an hour. So, instant water gardening—well, almost instant—is a reality for tub pond owners.

If the barrel is sunk into soil, moisture will eventually erode the iron supporting rings. Yet, few problems are likely to arise because the structure of the barrel, plus the outward pressure of the water, is likely to counteract any inward-acting pressure that may exist.

Stout planks, held in place by equally stout supports, can be used to construct a (usually) square or rectangular raised pond. Structures of this sort are not watertight, of course, and have to be lined. Not surprisingly, such ponds are not popular, even though, if properly constructed, they can last for many years.

CERAMICS

Ceramic basins or sinks can also be used to great effect for creating small water features. Though they can be used without pre-treatment, such arrangements tend to look rather unattractive. One solution is to coat them with an artificial mixture (details supplied in the section on pond construction.) The drawback here is that they need a drying period, followed by detoxification treatment (as for concrete) to render the coating safe.

ARTIFICIAL/RECONSTITUTED/NATURAL STONE

Other water features besides millstones fall into this category, e.g., pebble fountains.

All these systems have the obvious advantage of small size, which makes them suitable for small patios. One disadvantage is that the total volume of water required is small too. This could

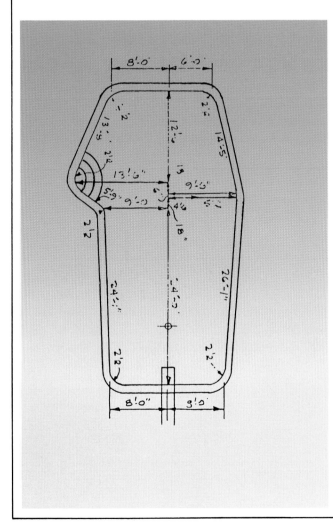

Left and Above: As can be gathered from viewing the various styles of construction and the various materials that can be used in construction, there are many possible roads for the garden pond enthusiast to travel; the options are only limited by your personal situation and desire. Remember, however, that no matter which road you choose, a garden pond is a rewarding and enjoyable way relax and beautify your home at the same time.

All ponds have their advantages and their disadvantages; the type of pond you finally decide on should be a compromise between your desires, the needs of the fish and plants, and the advantages versus disadvantages of the pond type.

Consider the purpose of the pond before choosing the materials to be used for its construction.

prove a problem because the splashing and recirculation of water which makes these systems so attractive results in considerable loss through evaporation. So the volume of water in the reservoir/pump chamber can quickly drop to dangerously low levels, particularly during hot, sunny weather. If not rectified, there could be permanent damage to the pump.

Some Advantages and Disadvantages of Various Materials

Concrete, Cement, Bricks and Blocks: Extremely durable; wide range of designs possible, from completely informal to formal; ideal for raised, formal layouts.

Some Disadvantages: These materials are not easy to work unless one is familiar with their properties and the relevant techniques; not ideally suited for use during hot, dry weather, or if frosts are a possibility; repairs are difficult to effect; lime is highly toxic—decontamination/sealing is essential.

Liners (Polyethylene, PVC, Butyl): Can be used virtually throughout the year; easy to use.

Some Disadvantages: Need to be hidden from view by plants, rockwork, etc.; wrinkles are difficult to avoid.

(a) Polyethylene: Inexpensive; flexible.

Some Disadvantages: Not very durable; sensitive to ultraviolet radiation; non-stretchable.
   (b) PVC (including laminated types): Strong; flexible and stretchable.

Some Disadvantages: Not cheap; not as durable as butyl and therefore not ideal for truly permanent features.
   (c) Butyl: Very durable; flexible and stretchable, but expensive.

Prefabricated: Shape predetermined; simple installation; very good for quarantine/treatment purposes, rearing of fry, tadpoles, etc.; safe for children to use; light to handle; available in formal and informal designs.

Some Disadvantages: May be small and/or shallow and, therefore, not well suited to winter

The obvious disadvantage of the tub pond is its small size. Most tub ponds are unsuitable for any but the smaller species of fish. The advantage of the tub pond is its ability to be placed in almost any size garden. It also has the potential to be moved.

survival; predetermined shape provides little flexibility.

(a) Plastic: Very light; inexpensive.

Some Disadvantages: Not very durable.

(b) Fiberglass: Durable; reasonably priced.

Some Disadvantages: Relatively few models are more than l8"(c. 45 cm.) deep.Some deep ponds of this type do exist though.

(c) Black Polyester: Very strong and durable; wider range of deeper designs than (a) and (b.)

Some Disadvantages: More expensive than plastic and fiberglass.

Wood: Easily available; long-lasting if designed for pond use, e.g., tub ponds; can be installed in restricted space.

Some Disadvantages: Can stain the water, can contain toxic preservatives if not specifically designed for pond use. (Tub ponds are, of course, exceptions); may rot if not of the right quality; will require lining (not tub ponds.)

Above and Below: While a high-spraying fine mist fountain can provide moisture-loving plants with the necessary water, such fountains tend to lose water to evaporation and will need to have the water level closely watched. The disadvantage of a small formal construction is that it is unsuitable for most forms of preferred inhabitants.

The above photo gives one an idea of how to combine various features of the garden pond. Here we see a wooden footbridge constructed beside a decorative ceramic figure, with a waterfall completing the scene.

Ceramics: Can be obtained cheaply, i.e., secondhand/reject basins or sinks; good for small patios, etc.

Some Disadvantages: Require coating to cover up 'artificiality'; sealing of coating essential; shape almost invariably rectangular.

Artificial/Reconstituted/Natural
Stone: Attractive and compact; particularly useful for patios, e.g., millstones and pebble fountains; easy to install.

Some Disadvantages: Not designed to accommodate fish or plants; high evaporation losses can quickly lead to dangerously low water level in small reservoir/pump chamber.

CHECKLIST OF EARLY STEPS AND CONSIDERATIONS

It will have become apparent in the preceding pages that the decision to install a pond cannot be based purely on impulse. It is fair to say that many of us (most?) start off by feeling some desire to own a pond. Unless a truly genuine desire exists, though, there is little point pursuing the subject any further. Although uncommitted people can, and usually do, grow to like their pond after it is installed, the risks of things going wrong can be high and, quite frankly, not worth taking unless the decision to proceed is firm. If the decision is firm, it should be followed by a consideration of several important questions. I should emphasize that the checklist which follows is intended as a guide and not as an inflexible set of rules.

CHECKLIST
1. Do you really want a pond?
2. If so, what type of pond, e.g., informal, wildlife, formal, would you like to have?
3. What range of plants, fish or other organisms will the pond be stocked with?
4. What are their requirements and characteristics?
5. Can these be met adequately in the space you have available for construction/installation of the pond?
6. If not, what is the maximum space that can be made available and what would be a realistic, revised stocking level?
7. Are the revised stocking possibilities

When you perceive the soothing beauty of a garden pond such as pictured below, you cannot help but feel the urge to design and construct your own garden pond.

If you decide to have a pond and wish to keep any species of fish or plant, remember that the needs of such life forms must have precedence over any whims or desires pertaining to size, style, or other factors of garden pond design and structure.

acceptable to you?

8. If not, what other types of plants and animals could be accommodated instead?

9. Having arrived at a reasonable stocking level for the available space, will the type of pond you now envisage be compatible with the pond inhabitants and your existing garden/patio layout?

Note: Native species in formal designs are not generally considered appropriate. Conversely, a wildlife pond stocked with, e.g., Koi, is a contradiction in terms. Informal ponds in formal settings usually look disharmonious.

10. Once a compatible combination of organisms and pond design has been established, what construction materials are most appropriate or desirable?

11. If, after considering all the above, your space still does not provide you with the type of pond you envisage, how happy will you be with the alternative?

Note: If you feel very unhappy, then a complete reassessment of the situation must be carried out. If no acceptable arrangement providing adequate conditions for the fish, etc., can be found, then the temptation to proceed regardless must be resisted. However desirable the concept of a pond might appear, it is far better not to have a pond at all than to have one that causes distress and hardship all around.

12. If no pond is possible, why not install a water feature such as a pebble fountain?

13. Even if a pond *is* possible, why not install a water feature in any case? These deserve full consideration in their own right, and could well have appeared near the top of the checklist (depending on your response to Question 1.)

Some of the points raised in the checklist involve a consideration of plant and animal species, stocking levels and other factors. All of these are described in later chapters and should be consulted in conjunction with the various items outlined above.

CHOOSING THE SITE

Much of the enjoyment that can be derived from owning a pond is inextricably linked with aspects such as its size, location and design. None of these topics are particularly difficult or complicated to come to terms with and a little time spent on them will repay rich dividends.

While personal preference may play a significant role in determining the exact location of a pond, it cannot be allowed to play the only significant role.

For example, it may well be that a property may have a rather unattractive north aspect which could well be 'lifted' by the presence of a well-designed pond. Despite this, though, siting a pond close to a high north-facing wall can create considerable problems in temperate countries.

When choosing a site, it is much to your advantage if you can make use of the existing components of the area, as for example the rock formations pictured in this photo. Also take into consideration the surrounding flora and fauna: Are there deciduous trees or predatory animals?

So long as your site is well-situated, there are virtually no limitations to your pond layout. The owner of this pond made use of stone purchased from a local stone distributor to create a lovely border that nicely complements this small, informal pond.

ASPECT

Light and temperature are the two main causes of problems associated with ponds sited close to north-facing walls, especially in northern latitudes. The trajectory of the sun is such that it is only directly (or nearly so) above the earth's surface around midday during the warmest months of the year. At other times of the day and year, its rays reach the earth at an angle. While the sun certainly rises in the east and sets in the west in the northern hemisphere, this is not the whole picture.

It would be truer to say that the sun apparently moves through the sky—it is the earth that rotates and creates the illusion that the sun is moving—from the east to the west in a trajectory that is tilted southward. Consequently, north-facing surfaces receive the lowest levels of illumination. This relative lack of light may be ideal for mosses, liverworts, ferns and other shade-loving organisms and may not even seriously affect plant growth in ponds during mid/late spring and summer, but it definitely is significant during the colder, shorter days of autumn (fall), winter, and early spring.

The absence of the sun's warmth-generating rays, or their relatively late arrival each day during the cooler months means that water temperatures will remain lower longer in ponds located close to northfacing walls than elsewhere. This means that layers of ice or snow will persist longer on such ponds, cutting down the amount of light reaching the water. Plants need light (some more than others) and can therefore suffer if the supply is inadequate. So the combined effects of light and temperature can adversely affect both plant and animal inhabitants of northerly-sited ponds. This is particularly true of designs that are on the shallow side, or contain less robust species of plants or fish, like *Lobelia cardinalis* (which produces brilliant scarlet flowers from late summer) or Orandas (twin-tailed fancy goldfish with raspberry-like 'caps' or hoods.)

Clearly, it is far better to choose a relatively open, well-lit site for a pond. One that can receive sunlight in the morning and in the evening and can also be protected from the sun's rays during the hottest part of the day during summer, is almost ideal. This

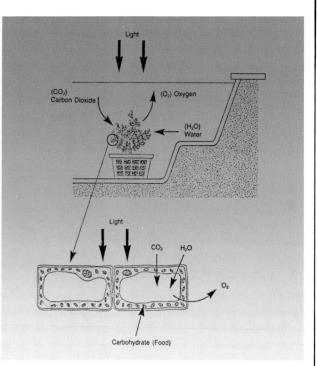

A very important consideration in determining the site of your future pond is light availability. All green plants need adequate lighting to carry out the process of photosynthesis. Adequate lighting will keep your plants healthy, which in turn will help to control the growth of algae.

arrangement is, however, quite difficult to provide. If you have some tall evergreen plants (not holly or laurel which are poisonous) and can site your pond to provide the above conditions, or if you can choose a position that is shaded at the right time of day by your house, then you can consider yourself fortunate.

In most cases, though, these conditions do not exist, so most of us have to compromise. In fact, if only people who can provide ideal conditions were allowed to have ponds, there would be very few pond owners!

Many open pond sites in built-up areas receive direct sunlight in the morning or in the evening and for most of the afternoon. During autumn (fall) and early spring, the water in such ponds is usually clear. But during the summer months most of them are susceptible to the algal blooms that produce green water—one of the unfortunate consequences of an open site.

Despite this, such sites are quite suitable since simple, effective steps can be taken to minimize or eliminate algal problems. Advice on how this can be done will be found later in this book (under problems, stocking with oxygenating plants and surface cover.)

Common sense is a most valuable quality when it comes to ponds. It will also indicate that cold spots, particularly frost hollows, must be avoided when choosing a site. Who wants a pond that becomes iced over every time the temperature falls to the freezing point when the problem can be easily avoided by choosing an alternative site, perhaps only an arm's length away?

THE PROBLEM WITH TREES

I have already mentioned that well-known double act, laurel and holly(!), whose poisonous qualities demand that they should not be allowed anywhere near a pond, even though, being evergreens, few of their leaves will end up in the water. Other plants which can be added to this

group are rhododendrons and yews. Among deciduous (leaf- shedding) species, laburnum (highly poisonous seeds), willows (produce aspirin) and horse chestnut (toxic leaves) should also be treated with extreme caution. Flowering plums and cherries can harbor the water lily aphid *(Rhopalosiphum nymphaeae)* during winter.

Quite apart from their potential direct toxicity, deciduous plants should not be grown near a pond (or a pond should not be sited near them) unless effective measures can be taken to prevent leaves falling into the water, or to remove them quickly and regularly if they do fall in.

The greatest danger with trees is the almost inevitable falling and decaying of leaves. This problem occurs especially in the autumn and winter seasons, when the leaves enter the pond and later decay under the frozen layer of the pond surface. Some species of trees are known to have leaves which are poisonous to pond life, and they are to be avoided at all cost.

The smaller the pond, the greater the danger of fallen leaves (or flower petals), as a smaller volume of water is less able to dilute a given level of toxic buildup.

Dead leaves will become waterlogged and sink to the bottom of the pond where they will gradually rot and release potentially lethal gases. In normal circumstances, these do not constitute a serious hazard to fish because gaseous interchange at the water surface will allow these gases to escape into the air. As soon as ice forms on the surface of the water, however, gases will be trapped under it and serious problems can then arise. The provision of an ice-free hole, as described later, will help reduce risks, but it is better to take steps to prevent the problem arising in the first place.

Leaf-fall, followed by rotting and release of toxic gases, happens all the time in natural ponds and fish appear to survive in them quite happily over winter. One could therefore be tempted to apply such rules to garden ponds. This would, however, be a total misinterpretation of the situation. Most garden or patio ponds are not natural and contain plants and fish that are not truly wild—most will have been bred commercially and, consequently, will not have evolved in natural conditions where natural selection weeds out the weaklings and gradually creates sturdy, resistant wild populations.

In addition, the frequent inclusion of exotic species, i.e., non-native, in pond populations means that, even if these were collected in their natural waters—which is most unlikely—they will probably not be ideally suited to survive in the conditions that prevail in their adopted home.

As a result, pond fish are likely to suffer more than wild fish from the accumulation of toxic substances released by the breakdown of an excessive leaf load.

Facing Page: Ponds and pools which occur naturally in the wild often have a constant supply of fresh water supplied to them. As a result, the life forms inhabiting them are in less danger of toxic buildup.

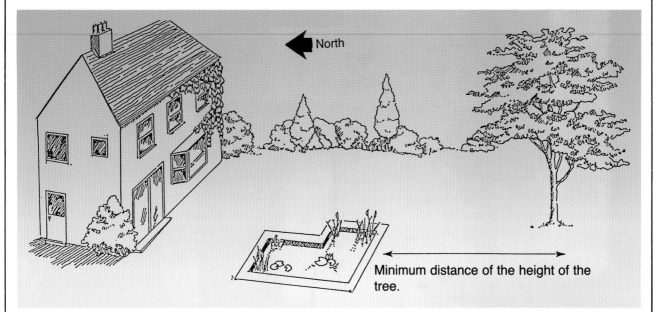

North

Minimum distance of the height of the tree.

SOME TREES AND SHRUBS TO BE AVOIDED

Species	Reasons
EVERGREENS	
Laurel	Toxic leaves
Holly	Toxic leaves
Rhododendron	Toxic leaves
Yew	Toxic seeds
DECIDUOUS	
All species	Leaf fall can lead to water pollution
Laburnum	Toxic seeds
Willow	Toxic leaves
Horse Chestnut	Toxic leaves
Flowering Plum	Possible overwintering host to Water Lily Aphid
Flowering Cherry	Possible overwintering host to Water Lily Aphid

Despite what I have said, it is possible to locate a pond quite near deciduous trees. You do not have much choice if that is the only site available. The problem of falling leaves can, after all, be overcome simply by using a net over the pond at the appropriate time of year, or by

This drawing illustrates one very important consideration in pond siting—the only truly safe distance between a pond and a tree is equal to the potential height of the nearest tree.

removing them several times a day when leaf-shedding is at its peak.

When siting a pond near trees, also consider possible root damage. There are no hard and fast rules about this, because trees vary so much in the type of roots they produce and the distance over which they can extend. To be on the safe side, allow a minimum distance between tree and pond equal to the eventual overall height of that type of tree.

Pond damage caused by tree roots is, at best, very difficult to repair. At worst, it will face you with two choices—either to remove the tree or abandon the pond. This is never a pleasant choice. Fortunately, this is another easily avoidable problem. You can eliminate root damage by cutting off all the main roots on the side of the tree facing a pond. But, quite apart from depriving the tree of a significant part of its supporting structure, and thus increasing the risk of a major catastrophe, trees which have lost some of their main arteries can quickly die. The risks are not worth taking.

Skillful planting and landscaping around the pond site can help alleviate damage to the pond life forms caused by strong or cold winds.

DRAINAGE

There is one area in which apparent common sense can lead to all sorts of difficulties—the siting of a pond in the wettest corner of the garden. It seems logical to create a water-filled hollow in such an environment, doesn't it? How wrong! Have you ever tried digging a large, deep hole in waterlogged soil or (worse) clay? It is not only messy, it is also next to impossible to shape a hole with mud-filled water splashing around your feet. Concrete will not set properly, if at all, under such conditions either. Nor can the problem be overcome by opting for a liner instead of concrete.

If the surrounding water table is higher than the deepest parts of the pond, liners can actually be pushed up from below by excessive water pressure, particularly when the water table rises after heavy rains. Inadequate drainage, combined with weather, can also lead to flooding. So there are very good reasons for *not* siting a pond in a naturally wet hollow.

SLOPING GROUND AND LANDSCAPING

Pondkeeping is so enjoyable and infectious that nearly every new pond owner will soon want a second pond or a wetland/bog garden. So, if you have a choice, it is always a good idea to choose a site that allows for future expansion. Obviously, sloping ground is not a good choice. In fact, steeply sloping ground can present considerable landscaping problems, even if no expansion plans are envisaged or feasible.

Gravity is a great leveller and ponds excavated on slopes are likely to have soil and rocks rolling down into them from surrounding higher areas, unless they can be prevented from doing so. Do not forget either that the soil removed during excavation has to go somewhere. One good option is to use it to raise soil levels elsewhere in the garden, or to create the illusion that the pond is in the lowest natural nonwaterlogged location.

This last point applies more to informal ponds which always look out of place if sited higher than their surroundings. (Raised formal ponds, of course, look satisfactory.) Skillful landscaping and planting around a pond can help overcome the searing of tender aquatic vegetation in spring by cold wintry winds. It will also prevent fully grown, potbound plants from toppling over later

on in the year. Therefore, if a convenient site, protected from prevailing winds is available, use it.

ELECTRICITY SUPPLY

All the points raised so far about the choice of site could be grouped together as 'natural'. All are connected in some way with environmental factors, such as light, temperature, and wind, or with the effects of the surrounding vegetation, such as leaf-fall and root damage.

Most pond pumps (available at your local pet store) will require an electric supply.

But few gardens or patio ponds are left to fend for themselves, as they do in nature. They are usually artificially serviced in some way by electrically operated devices. The watercourses, fountains, filters and lights that adorn our ponds, and can play such a crucial part in their survival, all require electricity. It makes sense, then, to select a pond site that is within easy reach of the domestic electricity supply. Waterproof electrical connectors are widely available and generally need to be used because, while most items of pond equipment are supplied with reasonable lengths of cable, few have leads more than 4 or 5 m (13 or 16 ft) long.

A well-constructed and creatively designed pond is so beautiful that siting it anywhere other than near a house from where its beauty can be appreciated is just a waste of much of its esthetic potential. Fortunately, the need to install a patio or garden pond within easy reach of a supply of electricity means that most ponds are sited within easy viewing distance.

THE FINAL DECISION

Before making the final decision on the exact location for a pond, do examine the intended site from various vantage points in the house. The view from upstairs can be just as interesting and important as that from a downstairs lounge. Only when all the viewing possibilities have been explored and their relative values have been assessed should the selected site be considered really final.

I hope I have shown in this chapter that the last thing when installing a pond is to be complacent about its location. Complacency and haste can lead to desperation in next to no time. On the other hand, patience and a little logic will work wonders and provide years of enjoyment.

A pond, once dug, is dug—a pond once built, is built! The feeling of despair associated with having to rectify a major early blunder is best left where it belongs—in the world of nightmares!

Patience and logic will work wonders and provide you with years of enjoyment of your well-sited, healthy garden pond. This drawing illustrates one of many such ponds.

UNSUITABLE POND SITES

1. North-facing Locations

Receive lower levels of light and experience lower temperatures than other aspects, particularly if the site selected is close to a wall or building.

2. Sites Near Trees

a) All Trees

If site is too close to trees, root damage to the pond can occur.

Minimum recommended distance: equal to eventual height of tree.

b) Evergreens, e.g., Laurel, Holly, Rhododendron, Yew

Some species have poisonous leaves and/or seeds.

c) Deciduous Trees, e.g., Laburnum, Willow, Horse Chestnut, Flowering Plum, Flowering Cherry

Leaf-fall can cause pollution, especially when pond ices over. Some species have poisonous leaves or seeds. Others can act as overwintering sites for certain pests.

*To protect it from wintry winds, a pond can be situated on the **south** side of a north facing wall. Remember, almost anything in your chosen site can, with a little ingenuity and imagination, be used to your advantage—and the advantage of your pond.*

3. Steeply Sloping Terrain

Soil and rocks will roll down into the pond unless they can effectively be prevented from doing so. Landscaping and construction can prove very difficult.

4. Cold Spots or Frost Hollows

Experience lower temperatures than most other sites, with the possible exception of north-facing locations.

5. Wet Spots (Below Existing Water Table)

Difficult to work in. Unsuitable for setting of concrete. Liners can be pushed up by water pressure from below. Prone to flooding during wet weather conditions.

6. Raised Site (For Informal Ponds)

Informal ponds can look unnatural if located on a raised site unless landscaping, perhaps using soil excavated during construction, can be used to create the illusion of 'lowering' the pond in relation to its surroundings.

SUITABLE POND SITES

1. Open locations (including those relatively distant from tall vegetation)

Receive high levels of illumination and warm up quickly—good for plant growth and health of fish. Algal problems that may arise because of high illumination can be controlled. Open sites are relatively free of leaf-fall and root damage problems. Midday protection from sun is desirable, but not essential.

2. Flat or Gently Sloping Terrain

Looks more natural than steeply sloping locations. Relatively easy to landscape and/or arrange to provide all-round viewing of pond. Makes all parts of the pond accessible. Reduces risk of rocks and soil rolling down into pond.

3. Low-Lying Sites *Above* Water Table

Most natural-looking sites for informal/wildlife ponds. Equally suitable for formal ponds, of course.

4. Sites Offering Protection From Prevailing Winds

Tender young plant growth is protected during early stages. Tall, fully grown/pot-bound plants will not topple over.

5. Sites With Space For Expansion

Allow for additional ponds, watercourses, etc., to be added later as pond fever gradually takes over and finances allow!

6. Sites Within Easy Reach of Domestic Electricity Supply

Facilitate installation of fountains, pumps, filters, lights and other electrically driven accessories.

7. Esthetically Pleasing Locations Close to and Viewable From Various Vantage Points Within the House

Provide interesting, differing aspects of the pond and allow viewing at all times, and in all weathers. Facilitate control of certain predators, such as cats, snakes, birds and children.

Above: If your pond is to have one of the many water features available, such as the fountain pictured above, remember that placement near an adequate electric supply will be necessary. A second consideration regarding location is the view afforded by the site. The above pond is situated so as to allow a pleasing view from the home and enough surrounding lawn to allow a leisurely stroll around the pond.

Facing Page: The construction of a footbridge which nicely blends with the surrounding environment creates not only a pleasing look but also allows one to view the pond and its inhabitants from above. If you take a careful and close look at the pond illustrated here, you should ascertain a good idea of how to begin such an addition to your pond.

2
Designing the Pond

By the time a suitable site has been selected, the decision about what type of pond or water feature is to be installed will probably have been made.

Ideas can evolve as construction and installation proceed, but all the main features of the final system should be largely sorted out before work begins. The following, at least, must have been decided:

- For which plants and fish is the pond to be designed?
- Is the pond to be formal or informal?
- If informal, is it going to be a wildlife pond?
- Is the pond to be lined, concrete/block-based, wooden or prefabricated?
- How large is to be?
- What shape is it going to be?
- If you have opted for a small design, is it going to be a millstone/pebble fountain or a tub/sink pond?
- Will fountains, pumps, watercourses, filters, lights or other features be incorporated into the design?

BASIC REQUIREMENTS OF FISH AND PLANTS

A pond designed exclusively from the human point of view will almost certainly result in hardship for the pond inhabitants.

Since the highest priority must be given to the well-being of pond fish and plants, it seems appropriate to include some brief details of their basic needs and how they can be provided for, so these can be taken into account at the design stage. Fuller treatment of some of these points is included later under various headings.

ADEQUATE OXYGEN SUPPLY

The vast majority of living organisms require an adequate supply of oxygen. In a pond, this can be provided by:

- An ample stock of submerged oxygenating plants, such as *Elodea canadensis* (Canadian

Green plants, such as Elodea canadensis *pictured above, provide oxygen during photosynthesis but deplete oxygen during respiration.*

Pondweed) or *Ceratophyllum demersum* (Hornwort.)
- A large surface area (some authorities believe 4.6 m^2(50 sq.ft.) to be the minimum)
- Surface turbulence produced by waterfalls, fountains or pumps
- Keeping stocking levels of fish within recommended limits
- Insuring good water quality

GOOD WATER QUALITY AND GROWING CONDITIONS

These are absolutely essential for the long-term health of fish and plants. Adequate conditions can be achieved and maintained by:
- Good aeration
- Installation of an appropriate filter
- Periodic partial water changes
- Selecting appropriate foods
- Not overfeeding
- Preventing toxic chemicals or excessive amounts of fertilizers getting into the water
- Preventing excessive leaves falling into the pond

- Maintaining reasonable plant and fish stocking levels
- Providing suitable growing media for plants
- Establishing a good overall maintenance routine

REASONABLE TEMPERATURE LEVELS

Extreme temperature fluctuations must be avoided. It is often not the magnitude of a change, but the speed with which it occurs, that upsets or kills pond fish. Excessively low temperatures can also prove lethal. Reasonable temperatures can be achieved by:
- Providing an adequate depth of water. (For permanent ponds, 45 cm (18 in) should be considered an absolute minimum. For Koi and other less robust species and varieties, even this is inadequate. 90 cm (3 ft.)should be regarded as their minimum
- Good water circulation
- Choosing an open site for a pond away from frost hollows/cold spots and north-facing sites
- Providing shallow shelves which can warm up in spring, helping early plant growth and stimulating fish activity

NOTE: Deep water, partly owing to its large volume, is a definite help in keeping algae under control.

APPROPRIATE SPAWNING AREAS

If a pond and its inhabitants are well looked after, spawning is likely to take place every spring and summer. Provision for this should be made by:
- Establishing relatively shallow areas, e.g. broad shelves, liberally planted with fine-leaved vegetation, such as Milfoil (*Myriophyllum*) or Hornwort (*Ceratophyllum*)
- Introducing artificial spawning mops or mats which can then be removed and the eggs hatched elsewhere
- Selecting good-quality breeding stock

To sum up, a pond (irrespective of what type of pond is chosen) that is designed for the biological needs of fish and plants should incorporate:
1. Large surface area.
2. Means of aerating the water.
3. Means of filtering the water.
4. Shallow shelves suitable for marginal plants.

A decorative fountain does more than enhance the pond setting—it also helps to aerate the pond water, as most gaseous exchange occurs at the water surface.

Even if your pond has extensive surface area and volume, water depth is still a vital consideration for the health of your fishes.

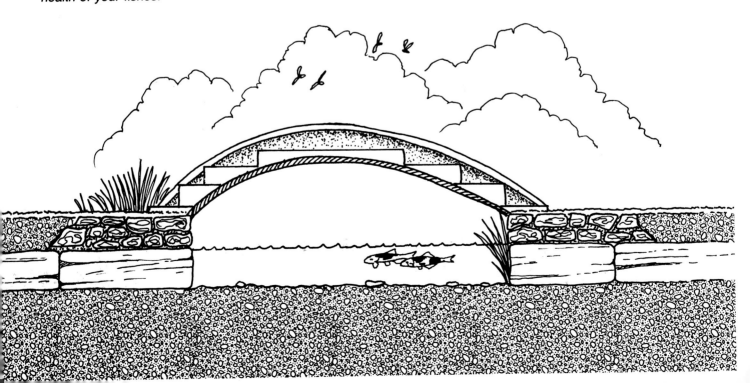

ORIGINAL SIZE

Of the above criteria, surface area, water depth and water volume together indicate that size plays a very important part in pond design. Though it is obvious that the larger the pond, the higher its potential stocking level will be and, consequently, the greater its scope for variety, there are other sound reasons for opting for the largest design that a chosen site can comfortably accommodate. Take two ponds containing the same number of fish but differing in size. The fish will produce the same amount of wastes in both schemes, but because of the relatively low volume of water in the smaller pond, the concentration of wastes will be higher. The larger pond, on the other hand, can cushion the adverse effects of dissolved and solid waste matter to a much greater extent. This, in turn, will benefit the fish.

GREEN ALGAE

Since the species of algae which are responsible for producing green water in ponds thrive on dissolved chemicals, it follows that the smaller hypothetical pond referred to above will suffer from this problem more often, and to a greater extent, than the larger one, particularly if the latter is also deeper.

In fact, if the two ponds have equal surface areas and differ only in depth, the smaller pond would suffer from algal problems much more than the larger one, even if no fish were present in either pond. One of the main reasons for this is that light will penetrate shallow water much more easily than deeper water. Algae love light, but they also love warmth, and shallow ponds warm up much more quickly than deeper ones. *Although there may be endless possibilities for your pond, some shapes are simply better than others.*

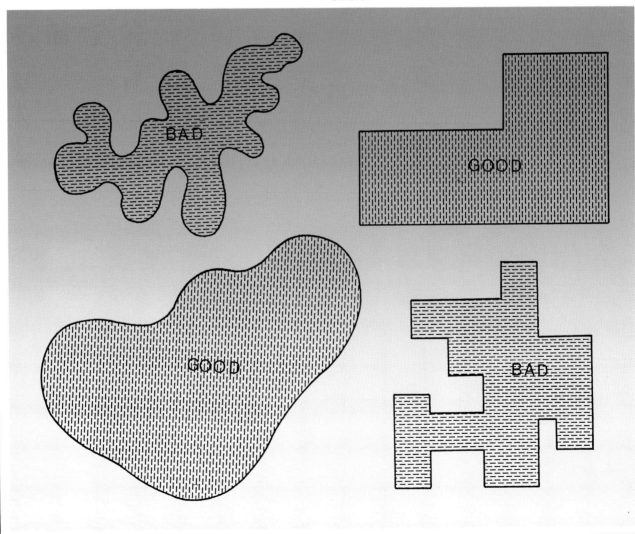

The result is inevitable—green water in a shallow pond, clear water in a deeper one, even if the surface dimensions are identical. Faced with this situation, some owners of shallow ponds will flush them out regularly with fresh tapwater to remove the algae quickly and effectively. In practice, this is only a temporary solution because the influx of mineral salts contained in tapwater is just what free-floating algae need. In no time at all, pea-soup conditions will have returned.

It is far better to take the behavior of green algae into account when designing a pond and go for the largest and deepest dimensions possible.

SLOPING SIDES

One way of constructing the largest pond possible in the available space would be to dig a hole, or construct a rigid pond, with straight sides extending to the full desired depth. Unfortunately, water expands when it freezes and, if this happens on the surface of a pond, considerable pressure is exerted outwards. Vertical sides may be able to resist this pressure if they are really robust, but there will always remain some risk of a fracture developing. For this reason, it is always recommended that slightly sloping sides be considered an essential feature of pond design. Slopes allow freezing water to slide

Whether your pond is informal (below) or of the formal type (above), sloping sides are beneficial in that they help alleviate the pressure exerted by freezing water.

No matter what type or size pond you choose—whether it is like the one above, those to the right, or of any other type—consider all factors prior to construction.

In fact, a straightforward uniform hole is not considered suitable even for most formal designs. Usually, something needs to be done to realize the full potential of the body of water being created. Large surface areas and maximum depth are not the only important criteria in pond design. Shape and shelf distribution are also important.

It is quite impossible to define the best shape for a pond.

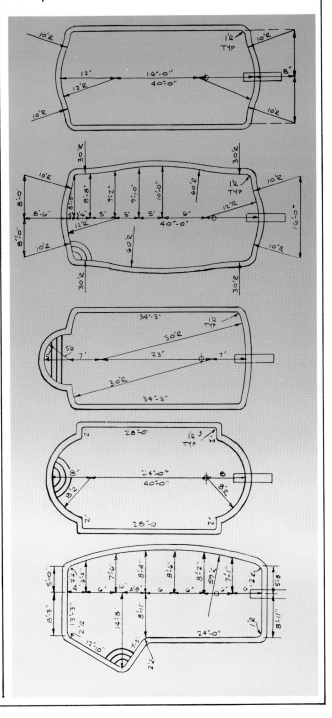

upwards, relieving or eliminating the risks of fracture.

If you have inherited a pond with vertical sides, the suggestions made later in the section on winter maintenance should help you. Because soils vary so widely, from clay at one extreme to sand or gravel at the other, it is not always possible to dig a hole with steeply sloping sides to a respectable depth all round. On average, though, a slope of 70° (i.e., 20° to the vertical) is possible in most instances. If a circular pond is, say, 3 m (l0 ft) across, a slope of about 70° would produce bottom circles with diameters of about 2.65 m (8.8 ft) at 45 cm (l8 in) depth, 2.52 m (8.4 ft) at 60 cm (2 ft), and 2.30 m (7.6 ft) at 90 cm (3 ft.)

However desirable the depth of such a pond might be, its overall shape would make it difficult to exploit to the full with submerged, floating and marginal plants. This may, of course, be perfectly in order for some formal arrangements but, if an informal scheme is envisaged, other factors need to be taken into account.

DESIGNING THE POND

Personal opinion plays such a fundamental part in this aspect of planning, and human tastes vary so much, that it would be pretentious and foolhardy to attempt to prescribe a 'best shape'. But some useful do's and don'ts should prove helpful.

A pond should be regarded as a permanent fixture in a patio or garden, so it is essential that its overall shape should be acceptable and pleasing to the eventual owners, and compatible with the surroundings.

If the site chosen is a patio, then formal shapes are generally the most suitable. Circles, ovals, squares, rectangles, or combinations of these, can produce a wide range of esthetically pleasing shapes. They fit comfortably into formal garden settings, highlighted by straight or smoothly curving paths, formal herbaceous borders and other symmetrical arrangements, and large expanses of lawn.

If, on the other hand, the pond is going to be located next to a rock garden or an informal wildlife garden, the shape should be made to look as natural as possible. Straight or symmetrical lines would look totally out of place.

One aim to bear in mind when dealing with informal schemes is that the pond should appear to have been created entirely by the forces of nature—as if the water had collected in an existing hollow without any human intervention.

If you take a close look at naturally occurring ponds, you will see that they generally have few narrow inlets. This should be reflected in our artificial ponds. A fussy design will create bottlenecks difficult to maintain, where water can become stagnant and encourage the growth of all sorts of algae, particularly the very awkward 'Blanket Weed'. It is far better to keep an informal design simple and open. It will not only look nice, but will prove easy to manage.

This last point applies equally to formal ponds. It is quite easy to devise a geometrical design consisting of narrow channels, sharp bends and neat cul-de-sacs, but keeping such a pond in good order is far from easy.

Since it is important to get the shape right before digging or installation begins, one should allow time to get used to the chosen outline. Various methods can be used. All work pretty well, so take your pick:

For patio sites, formal shapes such as circles are quite appropriate. The photo below illustrates a circular, formal pond with a centered island and a spray fountain.

A fussy design will often create bottlenecks or other problems; a simple design, such as the semi-circular layout depicted here, serves well the inhabitants and the owner as it is easy to maintain and keep healthy.

- The proposed outline can be drawn in sand on site
- Alternatively, a collapsible hose or wide tape can be used
- The shape can be marked out with wooden pegs joined by lengths of string or tape
- A scaled-down outline can be drawn on a piece of paper and examined at leisure

I invariably follow the second approach. I find that the width of the line formed by the hose or tape is substantial enough to be visible from a distance. At the same time, alterations, major and minor, can be effected with minimum effort and disruption. But this is just my way of doing things. Yours may be different.

The crucial thing, irrespective of which method you use, is to allow yourself time to live with the shape. After all, once you start digging, you are likely to be stuck with the consequences of your choice for years to come. It makes sense to allow a few days (less if you are in a hurry) to get used to your outline, adjusting it as necessary and viewing it from all vantage points.

TWELVE QUESTIONS TO ASK

Some questions which you should ask yourself during this stage of your preparation should be:
1. Is the design pleasant?
2. Will such a pond be easy to maintain?
3. Can the shape be appreciated from all the vantage points?
4. Is the pond accessible, near paths, the domestic electricity supply, taps, etc.?
5. If not, could the shape be altered to improve accessibility?
6. Is the design compatible with its surroundings?
7. Have you made allowances for landscaping around the pond?
8. Is the pond large enough?
9. Does the shape allow for a good distribution of planting shelves?
10. Will any of these obstruct the view from the best vantage points?
11. Will the shelves provide suitable sunning/spawning areas for the fish, and escape steps for dogs, etc.?
12. Have you allowed for expansion of your water garden, the installation of waterfalls, or lights?

SHELVES

The provision of shelves within a pond serves three main purposes. Firstly, they act as suitable planting areas for marginal plants (plants with submerged roots and aerial stems, leaves and flowers.) Secondly, they act as shallow sunning/spawning areas for fish. Finally, they enable a dog to escape if it accidentally falls into the pond.

Marginal plants can be found in the wild in water of widely differing depths. A great deal has

Facing Page and Below: When designing your pond, follow the examples illustrated—draw both a cross-section and a frontal view of your future pond. Doing so will allow you to better visualize your future pond.

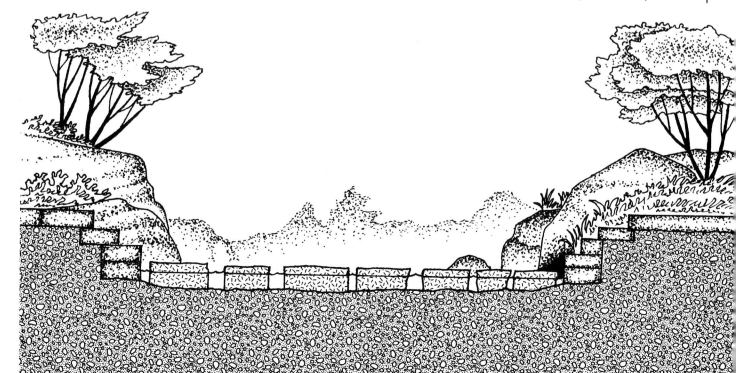

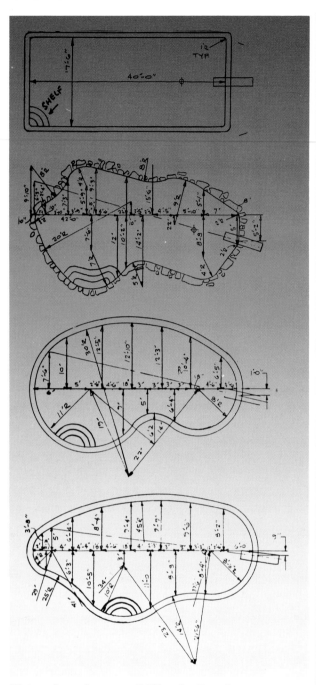

Pictured are four possibilities for the shape of your garden pond. The construction of a garden pond can be similar in many ways to the construction of a swimming pool. Indeed, these drawings represent potential swimming pools. If you have an idea or like an idea suggested in this book but don't feel that you can make it a reality, head to your local pet store to find out about a local pool builder who will construct a garden pond for you.

been said and written about the correct positioning of pond shelves in terms of water depth to suit as many marginal plant species as possible. The result of such deliberations is invariably a pond design of considerable and unnecessary complexity.

The fact is that most marginal plants are fairly flexible in their demands. There seems little point in arranging shelves at, say, four different levels in a pond that is only 60 cm (24 in) deep.

Experience has shown that a depth of 22 cm (9 in) and a width of around 30 cm (12 in) represent good working parameters for most marginal plants and even for some Water Lilies.

By supporting the plant pots or containers on tiles, bricks, or flat stones, a range of depths can easily be provided to cater for the needs of plants requiring shallower conditions. Those that require deeper water can be handled in a similar fashion by resting any supports on the bottom of the pond. It is not really necessary to complicate the pond profile by building shelves extending around the perimeter of the pond.

Desirability and necessity are two very different things. It could be thought desirable, particularly in formal designs, to extend the shelving all the way around the pond. This could improve the symmetry of the pond when it is empty, and make the installation of a liner simpler, but it will all be practically hidden from view once it is submerged. Anyway, the distribution of marginal plants in most ponds is usually confined to about a third of the total shelf area. Further, some formal ponds do not require perimeter shelving at all. If such ponds include plants that need shallow conditions, 'mini shallows' can be created at strategic points which do not necessarily have to be near the edge.

Ponds so thickly planted around the edges that the marginals occupy more than a third of the available space, can begin to look overcrowded, particularly if their surface area is small.

Wildlife ponds, despite their overall similarity in shape to informal ponds, differ significantly from the latter in that they do not require planting shelves of any kind. This makes sense. After all, a wildlife pond with a full complement of plants, in pots or containers, resting on predetermined shelves, goes a bit against the spirit of the wildlife concept, doesn't it? Wildlife ponds should

Through the use of rock formations, potted lilies, and other such things, a pond can have a soothing, natural appearance.

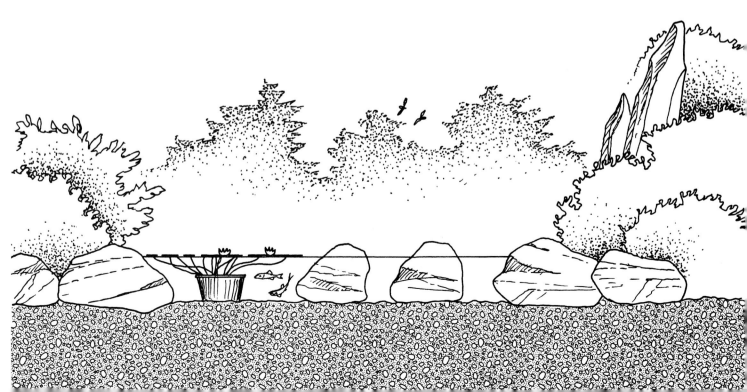

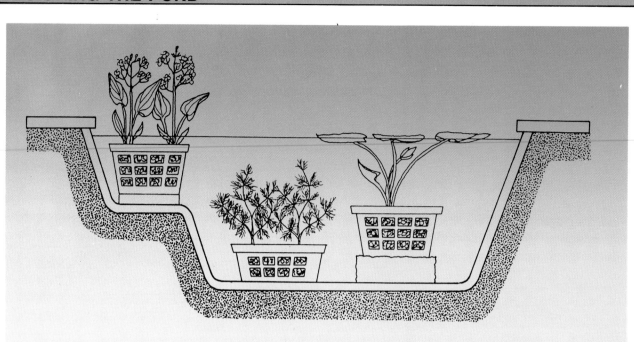

Marginal plants enhance the pond setting. Shelves for the placement of marginal plants should be incorporated into any pond design that is to include them. Planting baskets such as the ones in the drawing above make planting and plant maintenance an easy task. Such baskets prevent excessive root-spread and allow less hardy plants to be removed during extreme weather conditions.

attempt to imitate conditions in nature. One way of achieving this is by having a gentle slope covered with soil and extending gradually from dry land right down to the deepest point.

Looking at the profiles of the various designs briefly referred to above, we can end up with three very different situations:

1. A formal pond may not have shelves round its perimeter but could have shallow areas elsewhere.
2. An informal pond may have shelves, measuring about 30 cm (12 in) wide located at a depth of around 22 cm (9 in) distributed along about a third of its perimeter.
3. A wildlife pond may have no shelves at all, replacing these, instead, with a gentle soil-covered slope.

Of course, very attractive intergradations between the above can, and do, exist. As with so many other things, subjective opinion and creative flair can work wonders in exploiting possibilities to the full.

SOME FACTS AND FIGURES

Sides With the exception of wildlife schemes, ponds should be designed with steep sides. A suitable slope for most situations is 1 in 3, i.e., 1 centimeter (or inch) in for every 3 centimeters (or 3 inches down.) This is roughly equivalent to a 70° slope, i.e., 20° from the vertical.

Shelves Any shelves should be situated about 22 cm (9 in) below the water surface and should be about 30 cm (12 in) wide. They should occupy a third of the available perimeter.

Surface Ponds with small surface areas are prone to problems. Minimum surface area should be about 4.5 m² (50 sq.ft .)

Volume of Water It is difficult to work out the exact volume of water a pond can hold (except for formal designs, whose dimensions are accurately known), but the following figures are reasonable approximations for ponds with a maximum water depth of 45 cm (18 in) and a surface of 9 m² (100 sq.ft .)

Facing Page: With a little creative flair, a good knowledge of pond basics, a few pond accessories, and a well-chosen site, your garden pond can become a virtually problem-free water garden. Some such basics are shelves, surface area, water volume and depth.

Pond Profile	Approximate Vol. per Unit of Surface Area
Saucer shape, e.g., wildlife pond	22.8 liters per square meter (4.9 Imperial gallons per square foot)
70° slope with shelves	40.0 liters per square meter (7.9 Imperial gallons per square foot)
70° slope without shelves	43.0 liters per square meter (8.5 Imperial gallons per square foot)
Vertical sides	47.7 liters per square meter

These figures have been calculated according to the following approximate conversions:

30 cm	=	1 ft
900 sq.cm	=	1 sq.ft.
4.55 liters	=	1 Imperial Gal.

For ponds with a maximum depth of 60 cm (24 in), increase the totals by about 33%. For ponds having a maximum of 90 cm (36 in), double the given totals for a reasonable approximation.

Volume/Surface Area Ratio In general terms, the higher the volume of water per unit of surface area, the more stable the pond and the easier it will prove to maintain. The following figures can be used as a guide to the level of risk involved:

Volume/Surface Area Relationships	Level of Risk
50.5 1/m^2 and over - 10 gal/sq. ft. and over	Very low indeed
40.6-50.5 1/ 1 m^2 - 8-10 gal/sq. ft	Relatively low
26.3-35 1./1 m^2-5-7 gal/sq. ft	Acceptable at higher end, high at lower end
Less than 25.3 1./m^2-less than 5 gal/sq. ft	Very high

These figures emphasize the advantages of deeper designs.

Facing Page and Below: There is no rule stating that fish must be kept in any garden pond. However, if you wish to house fish in your pond, a balance must be maintained between fish and other life forms. As opposed to the pond below, the pond on the facing page clearly has an overabundance of plant life to safely accommodate most fish species.

As with all ponds, consider all your possibilities prior to construction. The pond pictured here makes use of existing rock structures. If your chosen site has an abundance of rock, gravel, or soil, try to incorporate these materials into your design as it may save both time and money.

REMARKS AND RECOMMENDATIONS

As the above text and figures show, there is no such thing as a perfect pond that will meet everyone's requirements and expectations. Yet, it is possible to make some general recommendations. It may not prove practicable to follow every one of them to the letter, but the closer you can get to them, the better off you and your pond inhabitants will be.

1. A pond should have the highest volume: surface area ratio possible for its size. This will minimize fluctuations and help provide a stable environment.

2. A pond should have the largest surface area possible within the limits imposed by the site. This should not be less than $4.5m_2$ (50 sq. ft.)

3. The shape of a pond should be pleasant, but simple and open, to avoid local trouble spots and facilitate maintenance.

4. A pond profile should be as steep as possible (though not vertical), except in wildlife schemes (saucer-shaped.) Aim for a slope of 1 in 3.

5. One level of 30 cm (12 in) wide marginal shelving should be provided at a water depth of 22 cm (9 in.)

6. A pond should not be less than 45 cm (18 in) deep. A depth of 60 cm (24 in) would be preferable.

If your pond is to be small and formal and is to house fish, it may be a good idea to add a fountain to increase the oxygen supply of the water.

The pond below is a small formal pond which has as its main focus a large stone fountain. While such a pond may be a beautiful addition to your garden, it is unsuitable to house most all fish and plants.

If your pond site is located in a natural area, try to work with the setting and keep the pond as informal as possible. Such should not prove difficult as many pond features are still open to choice. A fine example is the stone and earth footbridge construction illustrated above and below.

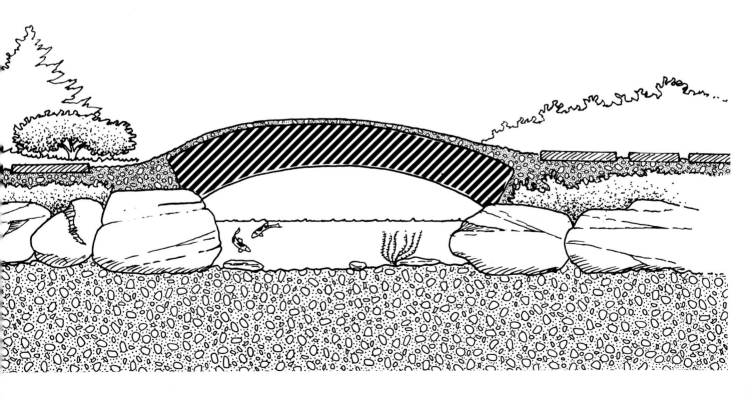

3

Constructing and Installing Ponds and Water Features

There are no inflexible rules restricting the construction or installation of ponds to specific months of the year, but a little thought will show that not every month is suitable for every type of pond.

Extreme weather should, of course, be avoided. During very hot, dry weather, soil, particularly if it has a high clay content, can become rock-hard and digging will demand an unnecessarily high expenditure of energy. The same is true in excessively wet or cold conditions.

Digging a pond is never the easiest of tasks and to me there seems little point in making matters worse by attempting (and probably failing) to become a martyr. Few people can cherish the combination of owning a pond and a broken back!

The construction of a pond which has cement and block as any of its parts will be limited by weather. Laying cement in excessively hot, dry, wet, or cold weather may result in present difficulties and future problems.

Prefabricated ponds do not suffer many of the weather related drawbacks of liners. If the weather is suitable to dig a hole, then in all likelihood a prefabricated pond can be installed.

MATERIALS

Other factors, mainly concerning the nature of the materials being used, need to be looked at too. While liners are flexible and can be used virtually all the year 'round, they can become quite stiff at low temperatures. When added to the considerable weight of some heavy-gauge liners, this can make handling and installation quite awkward. Further, if flexibility has been reduced by cold conditions, it can result in more than the usual number of creases developing in the liner as the pond is being filled. Yet, provided excessively cold days are avoided, lined ponds can be established satisfactorily at any time of the year.

Prefabricated ponds do not suffer from the same drawbacks as liners, so, provided the weather is suitable to dig a hole (or erect a raised support, such as a low wall), prefabricated ponds can be safely installed.

The pond season usually starts in earnest in spring, especially among newcomers to pondkeeping. Dealers are fully aware of this, of course, and, anticipating the inevitable rush for prefabricated ponds, they always stock up fully in late winter. As demand increases during the early and middle parts of the season, orders have to be placed on a regular basis with pond manufacturers and suppliers.

The peninsula construction here has many advantages.

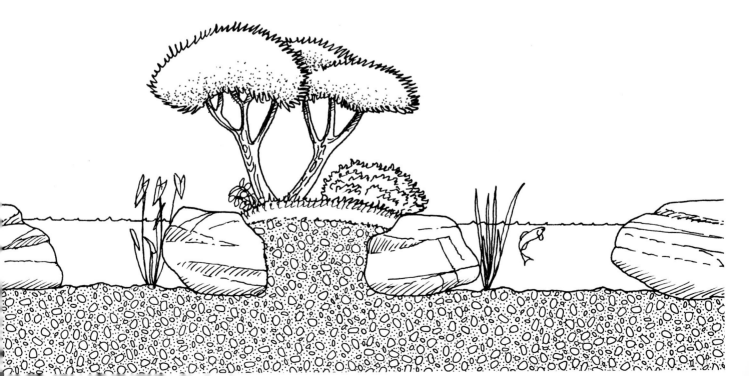

As the pond-keeping hobby keeps growing, the demands placed on masons, stone workers, excavators, and others increase. If your pond will need to use one or more of these tradesmen, it may be wise to contact them as soon as possible so as to avoid the seasonal rush.

Pond keeping is growing in popularity and technicality around the globe. This moat is part of an extensive koi pond in Japan. Japan abounds with beautiful ponds ranging from the simple to the vastly elaborate.

If, for some reason, the season then changes to become a bad one overall (usually because of adverse summer weather), dealers may find themselves with a surplus of unsold prefabricated ponds. On the other hand, if the season is a particularly good one, they have to keep their stocks as high as possible for as long as possible. This, again, means that, come the end of the pond building and installing season in late summer, successful dealers could still have a number of prefabricated ponds on their hands. Therefore, if you have not been able to buy and install one of these ponds during spring or early summer, all is not lost. You may even find that you can pick up one of these surplus prefabricated ponds at a fraction of the usual price.

If you obtain such a pond so late in the year that you are overtaken by harsh winter weather, all you need to do is stand the pond upside-down somewhere convenient until conditions improve. It is quite unnecessary to store these ponds the right way up over winter. This will only open them to potential damage by severe frost, snow and ice.

The construction of cement and block ponds needs more careful timing than that for the types dealt with above. There are several reasons for this. Firstly, the techniques involved require a level of expertise and familiarity with the materials that few of us possess in abundance.

We may all have handled cement and bricks at one time or other, but few of us will have tackled such a large job as constructing a pond. For most of us, building a reasonably-sized concrete or block pond constitutes quite a major, slow task. However slow we might be, though, we have to work fast enough to lay each complete coat of concrete in one operation, since joints are undesirable and often ineffective.

Two frustrating characteristics of concrete (from the uninitiated pond builder's point of view) are that it sets far too quickly and will develop cracks in hot, dry conditions. This clearly indicates that late spring and summer are about the worst times of year for building a concrete pond, unless you know what you are doing and can work really fast. Even an expert needs to be careful in extremely hot, dry conditions and will need to slow down the drying out process with wet sacking or some other appropriate alternative.

Frost can also wreak havoc with concrete, preventing it from drying out properly, causing it to crack and generally making life difficult for anyone foolhardy enough to try building a pond of this type in severe weather. Therefore, by a process of elimination, the best time of year for constructing a concrete pond is autumn (fall), when the air is damp but conditions have not deteriorated to winter levels.

One other tremendous advantage autumn has is that its relative lateness prevents the pond from being stocked until the following spring. This is quite fortunate because, despite its many outstanding qualities, raw concrete produces copious quantities of lime which have to be neutralized somehow, since lime is lethal to virtually every type of pond organism, even in low concentrations.

It is quite possible to treat concrete ponds with sealing compounds which prevent lime from leaching out and make it possible to stock them within a few days, but it is unquestionably preferable to give a pond time to mature before plants or fish are introduced. Autumn provides an ideal opportunity for this process to run its full course.

Several fillings, drainings, scrubbings and refillings, over several weeks, followed by a prolonged settling down period with, perhaps, a few bunches of submerged oxygenating plants thrown in for good measure, will convert a raw, lethal, concrete, water-filled, autumn-dug hole into a safe, mature, concrete haven in spring. 'Patience is a virtue...possess it if you can'—it will pay you and your pond fish and plants rich dividends.

TIMING CONSIDERATIONS

TYPE OF POND	COMMENTS
Lined	Spring is a good time for installing these ponds because water will mature quickly and a thriving community can be established in a relatively short space of time. Avoid very cold weather; liners become inflexible.
Prefabricated	Spring is a good time (see Lined Ponds, above.) Late summer bargains are often available. Avoid stocking till following spring if installation is delayed into autumn.
Concrete/Block	Autumn construction is best. Before hard frosts set in. Avoid excessively cold, or hot and dry, conditions because of adverse effects on the setting of concrete and development of cracks. Avoid stocking autumn-built ponds till following spring.

EXCAVATION

Whatever type of pond you choose, it might well be a good idea to consider hiring a mechanical excavator. This will take much of the back-breaking work out of the digging, particularly if your soil contains a liberal supply of stones or rocks. Even if you do not need an excavator, either because your pond is modest in size or your soil is easy to work, it is essential to decide beforehand where all the excavated material is to go. Remember that soil takes up a lot of room once it is excavated—certainly more than it did when it was *in situ*. The reason is,

Excavation, especially in rocky areas, may not be a simple task, but the end product can be truly fascinating. Slabs of rock can be rounded to form stepping stones or cut to form rustic-looking footbridges. The possibilities seem endless.

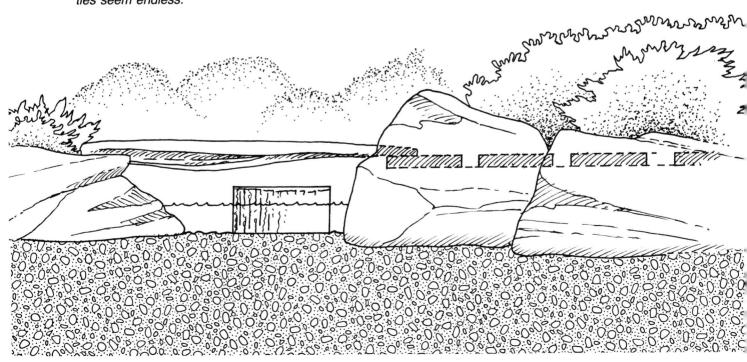

quite simply, that it is much looser when excavated.

Most soil profiles have at least two layers - topsoil and subsoil. The dividing line between the two is usually very clear, topsoil generally being darker, more porous, and containing fewer stones or rocks than subsoil. It is always a good idea to keep these layers separate when digging. The subsoil can be used later to raise levels or lay the foundations for landscaping schemes, and the topsoil can be used to finish things off satisfactorily.

LINED PONDS

The advantages and disadvantages of the various types of liner have already been discussed, but I would like to make a few points concerning choice.

CHOOSING A LINER

Always go for the thickest gauge liner available. Polyethylene should be around 500-gauge, used as a double layer for extra strength. Butyl should be about 0.075 cm (0.030 in) thick.

It is important to choose your colors carefully. Blue or black polyethylene is more durable than other colors. PVC is usually double-sided, e.g. blue on one side and sandy/brown on the other. Butyl is generally matt black. Unless a formal, obviously artificial scheme (perhaps containing Koi) is envisaged, blue is probably best avoided because it will show through the mulm and encrusting algae that normally accumulate and therefore looks totally out of place in an informal setting. Browns and black, on the other hand, soon mature, blend in and look quite natural.

ESTIMATING THE SIZE

It is very important to estimate the size of liner required pretty accurately before any digging is done. While you can cut an over-large liner down to size, this is wasteful and potentially very expensive. Underestimating the size of a liner could eventually save you money, but it will also leave you in an embarrassing and frustrating situation. Accurately reducing the size of a sculptured excavation can be one of the most soul-destroying tasks imaginable.

Your liner is going to have to deal with a lot of stress and trampling during both the installation and the subsequent maintenance and use; therefore, always choose the thickest gauge liner suitable for your purposes. In this photo, a layer of suitable pond flooring is being laid.

Above we see the opening moments of the filling of a pond which has a layer of suitable soil set on its walls and floor. When filling such a pond, you will inevitably encounter an initial murkiness; this, however, will soon clear.

Below is a drawing such as you should make prior to the purchase of your liner. If all variables are figured accurately, your drawing should enable you to determine the required size of the liner to be purchased.

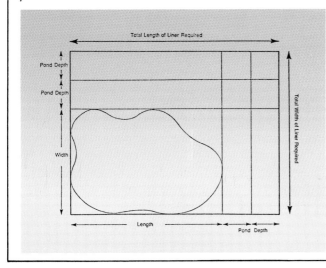

Yet, calculating the overall size of liner required so that you neither go over the top nor fall short is extremely simple.

1. Measure the maximum length of the pond.
2. Measure the maximum depth of the pond.
3. Multiply the figure obtained for the depth by 2.
4. Add this figure to the length obtained in Step 1. This will give you the length of liner required.
5. Measure the maximum width of the pond.
6. Add the figure obtained in Step 3 (depth x 2) to the width. This will give you the width of liner required.

NOTE: *It is important to remember that PVC and butyl are both flexible and stretchable, so the figures obtained above will provide sufficient liner to fit the hole and leave enough surplus to trim around the edges.*

Polyethylene is not stretchable, so, to ensure that you have enough material to tuck in under edging slabs, etc., *allow 30 to 60 cm (1-2 ft) extra all round.*

If the size of the butyl sheet required is larger than that normally available, or you need to add an extra section, special glues and tape are available. Butyl sheets can also be welded together electrically. It is clearly better to avoid

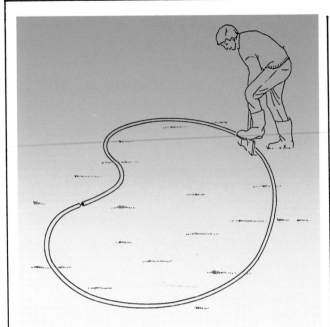

Before you begin excavation, mark carefully with rope, tape, hose, or other marker the shape to be excavated. Then proceed to remove the top few centimeters of soil within that outline.

having to do this, but it is comforting to know that it can be done if necessary.

EXCAVATING THE POND

Just as there are several ways of arriving at an acceptable shape, so are there various ways of excavating and sculpting a pond profile. The end requirements, irrespective of the steps taken, are nearly always the same.

A lined pond will generally require a deep, flat area extending over as much of the bottom as possible. A complement of shelves which will end up about 22 cm (9 in) below the eventual water surface will also be needed, and provision will need to be made round the rim for tucking in excess liner under soil, turf, slabs, or other covering materials.

Excavation should always start a bit cautiously, particularly if one is new to pond digging (it is now assumed that the outline of the pond has already been determined and is clearly marked out on the ground.)

Step 1 All potential obstructions should first be removed from the pond site. In a garden, these could be shrubs, bedding plants, or any one of a dozen other obstacles. Just because the site is

an open, sunny one, it does not necessarily mean that it has to be situated in the centre of your lawn. Demarcation lines between lawns and flower beds are, after all, often the result of subjective design, rather than of naturally occurring contours. The important thing is that the site should be reasonably level. If the pond is to form part of an existing patio, the chances are that the site will be covered with slabs which need to be removed and stacked safely elsewhere. It is also a good idea to remove one extra slab all round to create some elbow room for digging.

Step 2 Carefully go round the outline of the pond (on the inside of the shape marked out with hose, tape, rope or pegs) with a spade, removing the top few centimeters (an inch) of turf or soil in a strip roughly equivalent to the width of a spade. Once you complete this and have removed the outline marker, you will get a much more realistic impression of the overall appearance of your pond. At this stage, it is quite easy to alter the design and/or size, so make any minor adjustments you feel are necessary before proceeding any further.

Step 3 Cut back a further 30 cm (1 ft) all the way around the outside of the excavated shape to a depth of several centimeters (1 inch) to provide the essential rim ledges which will be needed later on for tucking in the liner under edging slabs. (Some people prefer to reverse the order in which they carry out Steps 2 and 3.)

Step 4 If your soil is very friable or yielding, you will almost certainly find that the edges will crumble into the hole as your excavation progresses. This will not only obscure the outline of the pond but can prove awkward to remedy later on. Further, ponds with insecure edges can be unsafe, particularly if they are surrounded completely by paving slabs, natural stepping stones with plants between them, or any other arrangement that will invite people to stand close to the water.

If your soil suffers from this potential hazard, you would be well advised to create a firm, concrete pond surrounding at this stage in the construction. All you need do is dig a trench about 15 cm (6 in) wide and no more than 10 cm

(4 in) deep all the way around the inside edge of the strip marked out in Step 3 and fill it with concrete, making sure that you create a steep slope of around 70° (the recommended slope angle mentioned in the previous chapter) on the pond side of the trench. This angle can be easily achieved with flexible shuttering, e.g. 'Lawn Edge,' in informal designs, or rigid shuttering, e.g., plywood (or equivalent), in formal ones. The shuttering is kept in place by bedding the bottom edge along the base of the trench, by the pressure of the concrete on the outside, and the pressure created by backfilling with soil on the inside.

The surface of the reinforcing concrete rim should be slightly lower than that of the surrounding terrain to allow the liner to be stretched over it and to accommodate the final layers of soil or cement on which the edging slabs will eventually rest. The concrete may find its own level if it is sufficiently liquid, but it is far better to spread it out evenly with a trowel, checking with a spirit level as you go.

Remember that water, unlike concrete, will always find its own level, so any mismatch, however small, left unrectified now will show up later when the pond is filled. Once the concrete has set satisfactorily, the shuttering and soil backfill can be removed and excavation can safely continue.

Step 5 Dig down to shelf level, keeping the angle of the slope as close as possible to the desired 70°, and removing any sharp stones you find on the way. The use of a simple hardboard or wooden template that makes it possible to check the depth, width and level of a marginal shelf, as well as the slope angle (at the same time), has long been advocated by experienced pond builders and water gardeners. This simple but effective aid takes only a few minutes to produce and is worth its weight in gold by eliminating guesswork and making life easier all around. (If you are building a wildlife pond without marginal shelves, then the angle at which you dig is, of course, considerably shallower and you can dispense with the template.)

Step 6 Having ensured that the shelves are level, continue digging down to a depth about 5

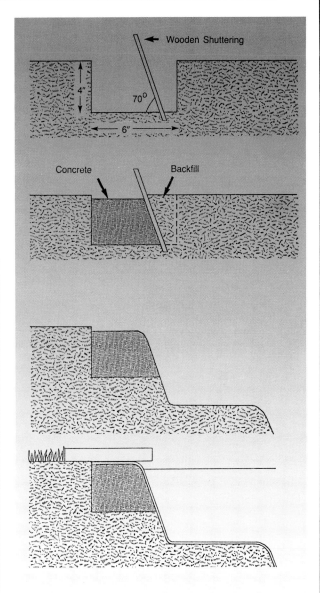

Following the four steps outlined above, it is a simple matter to install a concrete ledge. First excavate a four-inch-deep, six-inch-wide hollow; insert wooden shuttering at a 70-degree angle. Next add concrete; backfill to counteract the pressure exerted by the concrete. When the concrete has set, remove the shuttering and continue excavation. Install liner and secure with proper border.

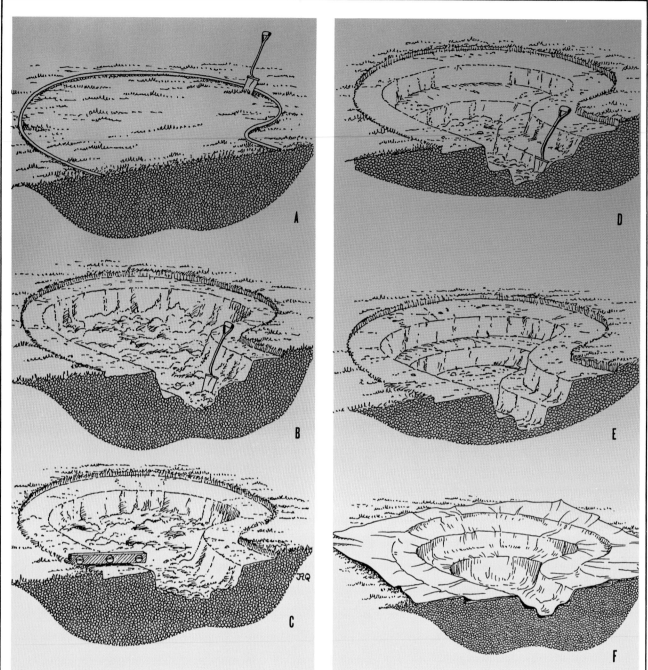

The excavation and installation of your lined garden pond is simple and easy if your proceed in a step-by-step manner. The illustrations above will help to show you how.
(A) Mark the excavation area and outline with rope, garden hose, or other suitable material.
(B) Excavate the pond area to the required depth, leaving an area large enough on which to attach the edging.
(C) Check to be sure that the shelving area is completely level.
(D) Using your spade, form shelves for marginals.
(E) Make sure that the base and walls are solid and level.
(F) Lay the liner across the entire pond area.
Note: Be sure the end of the pond has a sloped exit for distressed animals that might fall in.

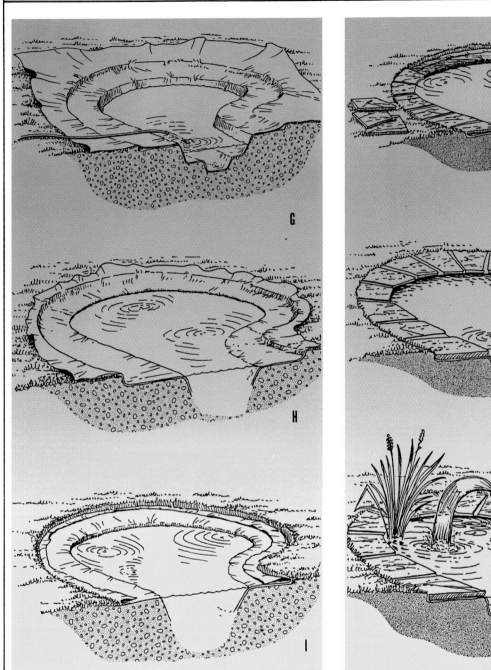

(G) After the liner is secured (bricks or blocks may help hold it in place) begin slowly filling the pond. The hose should be set at the bottom of the pond and the tap turned on slowly to avoid the liner moving out of place.

(H) When the pond is full, double check to be sure that there are no leaks and that the liner has not shifted.

(I) Using a sharp pair of scissors, cut the excess from the liner.

(J) Place the pond edging carefully on the liner resting on the edging shelf and secure it in place.

(K) Allow the edging to set and the pond to mature.

(L) Once the pond is safe for stocking, add fish and plants and enjoy.

You have successfully completed a beautiful work of craftsmanship.

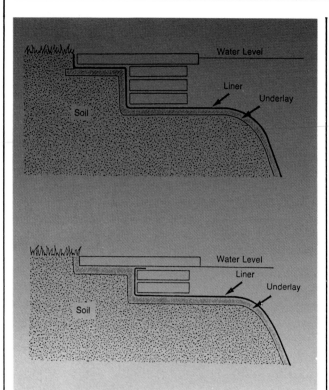

Your border stones should rest evenly on the liner, which in turn lies evenly on the smooth underlayment. The water level of your pond should never be above the liner, as this can cause seepage and erosion problems.

cm (2 in) beyond the desired pond depth. This will ensure that your pond will still end up as deep as you originally planned it, despite the 'base-cushioning' layers required. (See Step 8.)

As in Step 5, remove all sharp stones and other objects you find as you dig to minimize the risk of puncturing the liner later.

It may sound sensible in theory to provide a gently sloping bottom to the pond so that wastes and debris can roll down to the deepest point for easy removal, but this is not always such a good idea in practice.

If the pond is going to be totally devoid of plants, a gentle slope may indeed prove effective. This applies particularly to ponds specially constructed for Koi. Such ponds may also have drains incorporated into their design. But drains are probably best omitted from most lined ponds for other fish.

In the meantime, let's return to the inlusion or otherwise of a gentle bottom slope in the pond design. If you install containers or pots with Water Lilies, or simply add bunches of submerged oxygenating plants which will gradually spread, you will, in effect, create an obstacle course of such complexity that a gentle slope will be virtually useless. Most of the debris and mulm will simply be trapped by plant roots, stems, containers and any pieces of pond equipment (or support for these) that need to be placed on the bottom.

In such circumstances, only a relatively steep slope will work. But this is out of the question, unless some way of preventing containers from toppling over or losing their rooting medium can be found. It is therefore better to aim for a flat, level bottom in most ponds.

Step 7 Once the excavation is complete, it needs to be examined once more to make sure that all potentially dangerous stones, pieces of pottery, glass or metal have been removed. (It is amazing what you can find in back-garden excavation. I have even found a rusty frying pan 60 cm (2 ft) beneath the surface!)

Step 8 Digging may have been completed, but the hole now needs to be prepared to accept the liner. The usual advice is to cover the bottom and sides of a pond with a smooth layer of fine, moist sand several centimeters thick. This sounds quite sensible but theory and practice can (as they did in step 6) part company during this stage of pond installation. While it is extremely easy to lay a 5 cm (2 in) flat, sand bottom, plastering steeply sloping sides can be a very different matter indeed, especially during hot, dry weather when the sand dries out quickly and insists on obeying the laws of gravity with frustrating single-mindedness!

A second problem with using sand is that the bottom can soon be churned up as you move around inside the pond while plastering the sides. As a consequence, you could end up with areas consisting of a mixture of sand and soil dragged up from below, along with any sharp stones that may have previously lain hidden just below the soil surface.

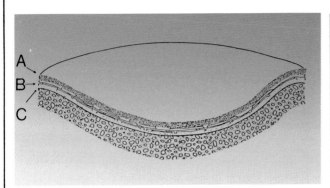

*(A) Clay/other suitable soil. (B) Non-toxic overlay.
(C) Liner.*

One final potential hazard is that sand can be scraped off the shelf edges and the rim of the concrete reinforcing surround, if one has been installed, by the pond liner as it gradually sinks under the weight of water when the pond is being filled. None of these problems arise with a saucer-shaped wildlife pond, of course.

Despite such drawbacks, a good deep, smooth and expertly applied covering of sand is hard to beat. If the soil is stone-free, some pond builders will use sand just on the bottom of the pond, the shelves and the reinforcing rim, making sure to drape some moist sand over the edges and leaving the sides either uncovered or else protected in some other way. Thick plastic bags, newspapers, felt, foam, carpet off-cuts, underlay, or any other flexible cushioning material, can be used for this purpose or, alternatively, as a pre-liner for the whole pond.

The important thing to aim for, irrespective of the materials employed, is to provide a complete protective cushion to ensure no damage will occur, either as a direct result of the weight of water pressing the liner against sharp objects, or by your body weight if you need to stand or move around in the completed pond during a major clean-out in the future. Butyl liners are very strong but they must not be abused.

Always wear soft-soled shoes or boots (divers' 'booties' are ideal) if you need to step into your pond at any time.

Step 9 Installing a flexible, stretchable liner is not just a matter of putting it in the pond and pressing it against the sides. This works quite well with polyethene though. Because of its relative lack of flexibility and its minimal stretchability, it cannot be installed using the water/gravity method outlined below, but needs to be smoothed into place before the pond is filled.

If the weather is cold, the flexibility of *all* liners is reduced, as well as the stretchability of butyl and PVC. In these conditions, it is always a good idea to leave a liner in a warm room for several hours beforehand to soften it. But avoid extreme heat. Certainly, do not rest the liner against a radiator, or permanent damage could result.

If the weather is warm, it is advisable to spread the unfolded liner out in the sun for a while. It will become more workable, making installation easier. It is also a good idea, once the liner has been softened, to roll it back lengthwise, just like a rolled carpet. If you then lay this roll along the side of the pond, with the free edge facing away from the excavation, Step 1 of installation outlined below could prove simpler, particularly if you get someone to help you.

INSTALLATION

Step 1 Stretch the liner over the pond excavation, ensuring that the overlap is equal all round. You may find it easier to stretch the liner over the pond if you place heavy, smooth-based stones, bricks or slabs along one of the long edges of liner to help anchor it to an extent all along one side of the pond. Two people can then pull the rest of the liner over the hole quite comfortably.

You will also find the liner will sag in the middle. This is fine, provided the tension is not so slack that the liner rests directly on a large section of the pond bottom.

Stretch the liner across the pond, making sure that the overlap is equal on all sides; placing slabs of stone on the liner may make it easier.

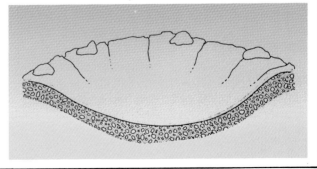

Step 2 Place heavy smooth-based weights at regular intervals right around the edge of the liner.

Step 3 Rest a hose in the cavity created in the center of the sagging liner and turn on the tap. The weight of water will gradually drag the liner down and mold it over the pond bottom, sides and shelves.

Step 4 As the liner sinks, adjust its tension by moving the perimeter weights in sequence. It is important to retain some tension at all times to minimize the size and frequency of the creases that will appear. Some creases will develop no matter how careful you are. They may be very obvious at this early stage, but they will tend to become less noticeable with time as the liner settles down and the inevitable encrustations of algae and covering of mulm and debris accumulate.

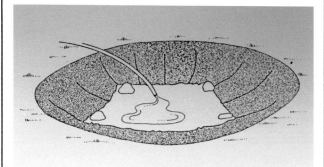

Rest a hose in the cavity created in the center of the sagging liner and turn on the tap.

Filling a pond in this way can take many hours, so you should not embark on this job until you can afford the time. Unless you can keep a check on progress throughout the operation, adjusting liner tension and generally keeping things moving smoothly, you are likely to end up with a badly fitted liner.

Step 5 Once the pond is full, remove all the perimeter weights.

Step 6 Trim off the excess liner with a stout, sharp pair of scissors or a carpet knife, leaving a strip about 15 cm (6 in) wide all the way round. This should be wide enough to tuck under edging slabs or their equivalent.

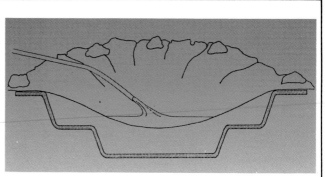

As the liner sinks, adjust the tension by moving the perimeter weights in sequence.

SPECIAL NOTE ON INSTALLING A WILDLIFE POND

Wildlife ponds are the closest artificial equivalents to the real thing and should therefore imitate natural situations. The saucer shape represents a significant step in this direction.

A further one would be to simulate the impervious clay/soil bottom layers found in the wild. But this is difficult to achieve on a bare liner, particularly if you adopt the water/gravity installation method described above. The rather slippery nature of the liner itself will not allow clay or other bedding material to adhere to its surface, so any attempt to cover a new lined pond with such materials is doomed to failure.

The following is one way of overcoming this problem and achieving as natural a situation as you can hope for.

Once the pond is full, remove the perimeter weights and trim the excess liner.

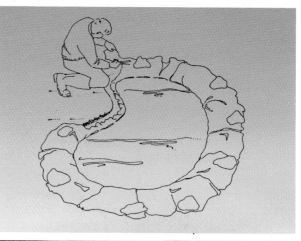

Step 1 Line the hole, using the same methods and materials described for 'normal' lined ponds.

Step 2 Drape the liner over the hole and smooth it into place, making sure it is in contact with the whole of the pond surface.

Step 3 Trim the liner edges as described under 'normal' lined ponds.

Step 4 Lay a complete covering of non-toxic material over the liner, making sure that you go well over the trimmed edges. (several layers of newspaper are ideal for this, providing a good non-slippery surface for clay/soil to adhere to.)

Step 5 Cover the newspaper with a layer of clay/soil several centimeters thick (an inch), pressing it down to avoid bare patches later on. (Even these will fill up in time, though, so you need not worry unduly if some appear after filling.)

Remember that wildlife ponds are the closest artificial equivalents to the real thing and should therefore imitate natural situations. The wildlife pond should probably be saucer-shaped and should house native plant and animal species.

Step 6 Lay a largish piece of liner on a fairly level patch of pond bottom (but within reach so that it can be removed later) and weigh it down around the edges with a few small, smooth stones.

Step 7 Lay your hose on the weighted-down piece of liner and allow water to trickle in gently to avoid excessive turbulence and turbidity.

Step 8 Continue until the pond is full, then remove the weighted-down piece of liner. (Despite these precautions, some turbidity is likely, but it will disappear after a few days.)

The series of photos on these two pages are of a wildlife pond owned by the Executive Vice-President of the company that published this book. The photos show changes made in the appearance of the pond as a result of seasonal weather variations.

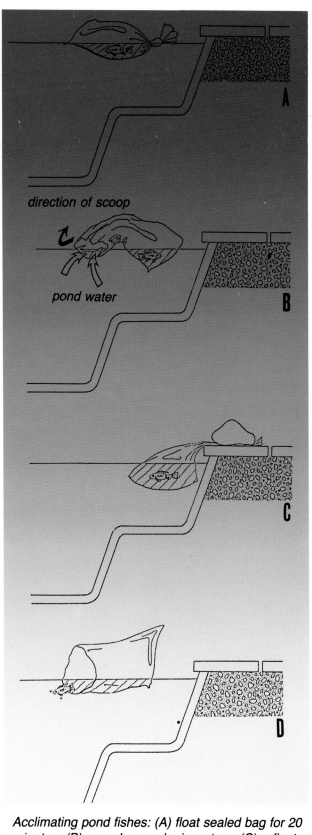

direction of scoop

pond water

Acclimating pond fishes: (A) float sealed bag for 20 minutes; (B) open bag and mix waters; (C) refloat opened bag for another 20 minutes; (D) release fish.

Checklist of Steps Involved in Installing and Filling Lined Ponds (see Text for Full Details)

A. SELECTING THE LINER
1. Choose appropriate color for the type of pond.
2. Choose liner of appropriate thickness and durability.
3. Estimate the size of liner correctly (allow 1-2 ft (30-60 cm) extra if polyethylene is chosen.)

B. DIGGING THE POND
1. Remove obstructions from pond site.
2. Excavate the pond outline.
3. Excavate the rim ledges.
4. Build reinforcing concrete surround if necessary.
5. Dig down to shelf level (not necessary in wildlife ponds.)
6. Remove stones and other sharp objects.
7. Continue digging down to ultimate pond depth, plus 2 in (5 cm.)
8. Create gentle bottom slope if necessary.
9. Repeat Step 6.
10. Prepare excavation to receive liner using sand or other suitable cushioning materials.

C. INSTALLING THE LINER/FILLING THE POND
1. FORMAL AND INFORMAL PONDS
   a. Maximize 'workability' of liner by leaving in a warm room or spreading out in the sun for several hours.
   b. Roll up liner lengthwise.
   c. Lay down liner alongside pond with free edge directed away from excavation.
   d. Weigh down free edge of liner with smooth-based stones, bricks or slabs.
   e. Using two people, gradually unroll and stretch liner over the pond ensuring equal overlaps all around.
   f. Weigh down edges of liner right around the pond (as in 4), ensuring that amount of sag is not excessive.
   g. Rest a hose in 'central cavity' of liner and turn on the tap.
   h. Allow weight of water to drag liner gently downwards molding it against pond sides and bottom.

i. Adjust perimeter weights as needed.

j. Once pond is full, remove all perimeter weights.

k. Trim off excess liner to within 6 in (l5 cm) of pond edge.

2. WILDLIFE PONDS

   a. Follow Steps 1-3 as above.

   b. Smooth liner into position inside pond.

   c. Trim off excess liner to within 6 in (15 cm) of pond edge.

   d. Cover liner completely with non-toxic material, e.g. thick layers of newspaper, ensuring that pond edges are overlapped.

   e. Cover pond profile with a layer of clay/soil approximately 2 in (5 cm) thick.

   f. Lay a square sheet of liner on a flat area of pond bottom, within easy reach of edge.

   g. Weigh down liner sheet with small rounded stones.

   h. Rest hose on liner sheet and gently turn on tap.

   i. When pond is full, remove liner sheet.

The layout and construction of an informal pond will vary slightly from that of a formal or even a wildlife pond. You must conclusively decide upon the type of pond before purchase and installation.

Ponds naturally occurring in the wild are shaped and determined by forces other than man. The consequential inhabitants occur and survive because they are best adapted to the given environment.

Contrary to the belief of some, the installation of a prefabricated pond does not prevent the addition of features such as waterfalls.

4
Prefabricated Ponds

Prefabricated ponds overcome one of the problems of pond design that some people find quite difficult, i.e., creating an attractive, original shape. They are also, obviously, more resistant than liners to puncturing and have the added advantage of making raised schemes possible. Although raised, lined ponds are feasible, such designs are rare and usually restricted to wooden-walled ponds or to previously existing concrete ponds that have developed major leaks which are difficult to repair.

The inherent rigidity of the materials used in prefabricated ponds makes it unnecessary to match the shapes of the excavation and the pond as accurately as more flexible materials demand. However, support must be provided for the shelves, where necessary, to prevent undue stresses developing when the pond is filled.

On the debit side, the mere fact that the shape is predetermined may be seen as a major drawback by those who like to decide the shape of a pond, its size and depth, and the distribution of shelves, for themselves.

Until quite recently, most prefabricated ponds were relatively small and shallow. As pointed out elsewhere, water depth is a key factor in the survival of most pond plants and all fish where winters are harsh. Over the past few years, though, prefabricated ponds 4-5 ft (120-125 cm) deep have become more readily available. While a depth of more than 2 ft (60 cm) is usually not vital for most organisms during winter, some of the more delicate, man-made varieties of Goldfish and Koi do appear to benefit from it. Children's swimming and wading pools should be investigated for larger prefabricated ponds.

INSTALLING SUNKEN PREFABRICATED PONDS

All the considerations about choice of site described for other ponds apply equally to prefabricated designs, with one significant difference about the excavation. While it is quite easy (within limits) to fit a liner or wet concrete

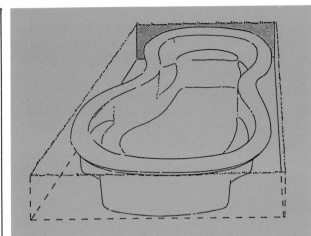

Once the site for the specific pond has been determined, a measurement is taken to determine the area to be excavated.

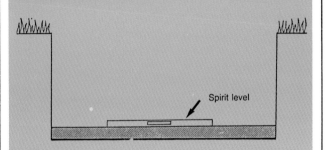

After digging the hole, removing all large stones, and compacting the soil, make sure that the bottom is level.

Insert the pond and support it with blocks, to make sure that the pond is level and secure.

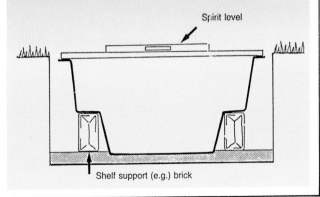

into a hole, irrespective of its depth or profile, the same cannot be said of a prefabricated pond. Since its shape is predetermined, one would need the mind of a computer to excavate a profile to match the contours of such a pond accurately. Fortunately, this is quite unnecessary, even though some manufacturers have been known to recommend as close a match as possible between pond and excavation. Installation techniques can vary, but the following has proven particularly successful.

Step 1 Invert the pond and rest it on the chosen site.

Step 2 Mark out a rectangle that will encompass the maximum length and width of the pond. If the pond is narrower at one end than at the other, mark out a 'tapering' shape instead.

Step 3 Excavate a hole about 9 in (22 cm) longer and wider than the marked out shape and about 2 in (5 cm) deeper than the deepest section of the pond.

Step 4 Remove any large stones or other obvious and potentially hazardous objects from the hole.

Step 5 Compact the soil all around the bottom of the excavation.

Step 6 Cover the bottom with cushioning material (as in lined ponds.) Sand is particularly useful because it can be molded around the pond bottom to form a firm base.

Step 7 Fit the pond into the excavation, taking care to set the bottom firmly in the sand.

Step 8 Support the shelves and the shallow end of the pond with bricks or blocks.

Step 9 Ensure that the pond is absolutely level from end to end and side to side, and that the rim lies several centimeters *below* the surrounding terrain. The exact amount allowed should take account of the thickness of the surrounding edging slabs (if some are to be incorporated in the design), and the fact that the pond will actually rise by a few centimeters as a result of **Step 10.**

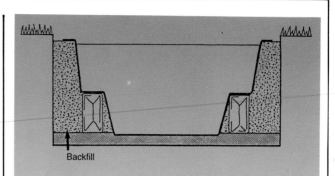

Once the pond is secure and level, backfill to the top of the pond. Backfilling will help counteract the pressure exerted by the water.

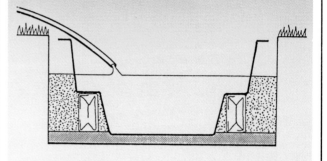

Once backfilling is complete, begin to slowly fill the pond. Keep an eye on potential problems such as the pond's shifting as a result of the increased pressure.

Step 10 Backfill the space between the pond and the excavation with some of the soil dug out earlier, if this is in reasonable condition. If it is of very poor quality or extremely stony, discard it and use sand or good quality (e.g., sifted) soil instead. Compress the backfill as you go along to ensure maximum support and eliminate risks of subsidence later on.

To avoid excessive inwardly directed pressure on the shelf itself, you can fill the pond at the same time as you carry out the backfilling, keeping the level of the water and the backfill approximately equal as you go. If it proves possible to compact sand/soil snugly under the shelves, this should be done to provide all around, even support. (The bricks or blocks used in **Step 8** can be removed in this case if desired.)

INSTALLING RAISED PREFABRICATED PONDS

Despite numerous advantages, sunken prefabricated ponds suffer from the same drawbacks as all other sunken ponds. They are liable to collect large numbers of wind-blown leaves (particularly in autumn) and a regular sprinkling of trimmings every time the lawn is mowed.

These and other problems (like children falling in!) can be avoided by installing a raised pond. It is sometimes suggested that all one need to do is rest the pond on the selected spot, support the shelves with bricks or blocks (as with sunken prefabricated ponds) and build a wall round it. This can be done, and can even prove quite successful, especially since it makes it possible to lift the pond out every time it needs a good scrub.

But one main disadvantage of this technique is that it may leave largish areas unsupported and not strong enough for *in situ* cleaning when you need to step into the pond. Far better, I think, is to take a little extra time and care, as suggested below. This technique results in a stable, safe, raised pond.

Step 1 Mark out a rectangle or other shape roughly equivalent to the overall size of the lowest shelf level.

Step 2 Excavate a hole about 9 in (22 cm) longer and wider than the marked out shape and about 2 in (5 cm) deeper than the height between the lowest shelf level and the pond bottom.

Step 3 Remove any large stones or other potentially dangerous objects from the excavation.

Step 4 Compact the soil on which the pond bottom will rest.

Step 5 Cover the bottom of the excavation with a layer of cushioning material, such as sand, about 2 in (5 cm) thick.

Step 6 Fit the pond base into the excavation and press it down firmly to 'bed it in', checking that the pond is absolutely level from end to end and

(A) Determine and mark a rectangle or other shape prior to construction.

(B) After excavation, remove any large stones, compact soil, and ensure that the bottom is level.

(C) Insert the pond, backfill for support, and be certain that the pond is level. Support the pond sides that are above the surface with blocks and backfill.

The following series of drawings is designed to illustrate the basic steps required for the installation of a raised prefabricated pond.

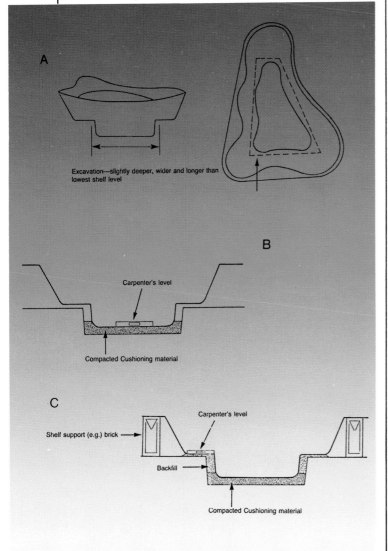

A

Excavation—slightly deeper, wider and longer than lowest shelf level

B

Carpenter's level

Compacted Cushioning material

C

Shelf support (e.g.) brick

Carpenter's level

Backfill

Compacted Cushioning material

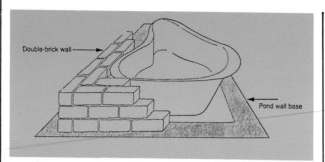

Compress the soil on which the wall is to rest; ensure that it is level. Construct the wall using the proper materials.

from side to side. (It is not necessary to allow for the pond to rise as described in **Step 9** on sunken pond installation.)

Step 7 Backfill the space between the pond and the excavation with some of the soil dug up earlier, or with sand if the soil is unsuitable, being sure to press it firmly all the way around as you proceed. Continue backfilling until the lowest shelf level is supported evenly all along its length.

Step 8 Check your levels once more and make any necessary adjustments.

Step 9 Support any remaining shelf levels with bricks or blocks.

Step 10 If the pond is being installed in an existing patio, there may well be a firm base on which the surrounding wall can be built. If not, then a firm concrete base has to be created. Either way, mark out the base of the wall. This should be far enough from the pond rim to allow you to install edging slabs later on. If you do not need to create a firm base, omit **Step 11** and proceed to **Step 12.**

Step 11 Dig a trench several centimeters wider than the marked-out base of the wall and about 8 in (20 cm) deep all the way around the pond. Fill this with a layer of concrete 5-6 in (12-15 cm) thick and allow it to set (allow about one day) before proceeding to **Step 12.** The concrete mixture should consist of 3 parts coarse aggregate (stone chippings): 2 parts sharp sand : 1 part cement, mixed into a firm consistency with water.

If the pond is very large, or if the wall is going to be very high, you may wish to provide firmer foundations. If so, dig your trench approximately 4 in (10 cm) deeper than indicated above and fill this space with compacted hardcore. Smashed up old bricks and stone debris are perfectly satisfactory. Follow this with the concrete layer as described.

Note that the trench is deeper in both cases than the wall foundations themselves. This is intentional and will result in the first row of bricks/blocks being half submerged in the finished wall. Besides making the base of the wall more rigid, this can look quite attractive.

Step 12 Build the wall to the desired height with pre-soaked blocks or bricks, interlocking them as described in the section on block ponds and checking your levels frequently. The wall should be of double-brick width. Anything less could prove too weak in the long run. Extra strength (if desired) can be provided by leaving a small gap between the outer and inner layer of bricks and filling this with cement. Use a cement mixture of 3 parts sharp sand to 1 part cement.

Step 13 Allow the wall to set properly for a few days. Protect the drying cement during hot, dry weather with moist sacking. In very cold weather, use a small amount of 'cement anti-freeze' in your mixture and cover your work up with plastic sheets at night.

Backfill around the wall to add further support and then complete the construction by setting the border across the top of the pond and the pond wall.

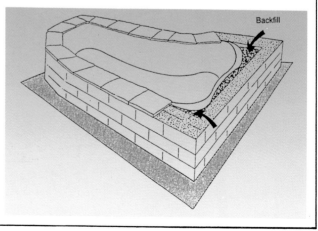

Step 14 Once the cement has set completely, backfill the space between the wall and the pond with compacted soil or sand as described earlier, making sure that the pond rim is particularly well supported. Remember that this edge will have to take the weight of the edging slabs, plus the weight of any admirers who succumb to temptation and decide to use it as a seat.

CHECKLIST OF STEPS INVOLVED IN INSTALLING PREFABRICATED PONDS

A. EXCAVATING THE POND

1) Sunken Ponds
   a. Invert pond on selected site.
   b. Mark out rectangular shape large enough to encompass whole pond.
   c. Excavate hole 9 in (22 cm) larger than rectangle and 2 in (5 cm) deeper than pond.
   d. Clear excavation of large stones.

2) Raised Ponds
   a. Mark out rectangle or other shape roughly equivalent in size to lowest shelf level.
   b. Excavate hole 9 in (22 cm) larger than marked-out shape and 2 in (5 cm) deeper than height between lowest shelf level and pond bottom.
   c. Clear excavation of large stones.

B. INSTALLING THE POND

1) Sunken Ponds
   a. Compact bottom of excavation.
   b. Cover bottom of excavation with cushioning material.
   c. Fit pond into excavation.
   d. Support shelves.
   e. Check levels ensuring that pond rim is slightly below surrounding terrain.
   f. Backfill perimeter space and compact soil as you proceed. (Inwardly directed pressure may be counteracted by filling pond with water at approximately the same rate as backfilling is progressing.)

2) Raised Ponds
   a. Follow **Steps 1-3** as above.
   b. Check levels.
   c. Backfill perimeter space and compact soil as you proceed.
   d. Support exposed shelves.
   e. Create firm wall base if one is necessary. (See **Step 11** of installation procedure in main text.)
   f. Construct wall, checking levels regularly, ensuring that final row is in line with pond rim, and allowing sufficient space between wall and pond rim to accommodate edging slabs.
   g. Backfill space between wall and pond with compacted soil.

Whether prefabricated, cement and block, lined, natural, or of other construction, a garden pond is a handsome addition to any garden.

5

Concrete and Cement Ponds

Although it is quite possible to construct raised concrete ponds, most are of the sunken type. Some raised ponds that look as if they were built of concrete are, in fact, block ponds whose walls are completely coated on the inside and the outside with a rendering of cement.

The heading at the top of this chapter truly reflects the potentially misleading terminology associated with this type of pond. While the bulk of the base and sides of a 'concrete' pond are, indeed, made up of concrete, the top coats always consist of cement, with no coarse aggregate in the final mixture. Therefore a concrete pond is usually a hybrid between concrete and cement. When properly constructed and designed, such a pond lasts virtually forever. Powerful evidence of this can be found in the old ponds of established stately homes and palaces the world over. Pond builders of bygone days may not have had the choice of materials we have today (with all their built-in advantages) but they certainly knew how to make the most of the few materials they did have. In fact, some of these old ponds still look as good, permanent and impressive as they must have done the day they were completed.

When properly constructed, a concrete and block pond will last virtually forever.

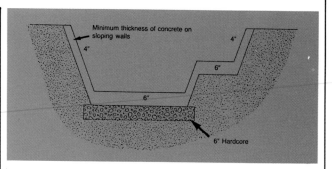

Constructing a concrete pond will require basic knowledge of masonry. Allowance must be made for a six-inch thick base and four-inch thick walls. The pond should rest on six-inch-thick hardcore.

CONSTRUCTING A CONCRETE POND

Excavating a concrete pond is done along the same lines detailed for lined ponds, except that allowances have to be made for a base measuring about 6 in (15 cm) thick and sloping sides of at least 4 in (10 cm.) If the sides are to be vertical, then they should be at least 6 in (15 cm) thick, like the base. The depth of the excavation should also include, if possible, a layer of compacted hardcore about 6 in (15 cm) thick.

Once all this has been provided for, construction can begin as follows.

Step 1 Cover the base of the excavation with hardcore (crushed stones or bricks) and compact this into a layer 6 in (15 cm) thick.

Step 2 Make up a *dry* mixture of concrete consisting of 3 parts coarse aggregate; 2 parts sharp sand; 1 part cement. Mix thoroughly.

Step 3 Add sufficient water to form a consistency that allows a slit made with a spade to remain open.

Step 4 If the pond is small, combine **Steps 5** and **7** into a single operation. If the pond is large, follow **Step 5, 6** and **7** separately.

Step 5 INFORMAL PONDS—Lay concrete along base and around the sides of the pond to a depth of about 2½ in (6 cm.)

Step 5 FORMAL PONDS—Lay concrete only along the base of the pond to a depth of about 2½ in (6 cm.)

Step 6 INFORMAL PONDS—Cover base and sides with a layer of heavy gauge chicken wire to provide extra reinforcement. Steel mesh or rods may be used if the pond is very large.

Step 6 FORMAL PONDS—Use chicken wire only on the base, with rods or mesh being installed later when the pond sides are constructed.
   NOTE: *Either way, bed the chicken wire into the concrete to ensure that no exposed areas protrude after* **Step 7** *is completed. Exposed bits of wire will obviously rust quickly and cause serious problems later.*

Step 7 INFORMAL PONDS—Lay the remaining concrete to a total depth of about 5 in. (l2 cm) along the base and 3 in (8 cm) on the sloping sides and shelves.

Step 7 FORMAL PONDS—Finish laying the base to a depth of 5 in (12 cm) but only if shuttering **(Step 8)** can be installed immediately. Otherwise, do not complete base but 'key' the surface instead to ensure an effective join when the final layer of concrete is added later on.

A concrete pond base is composed of layers of concrete, reinforcement, and a second layer of concrete. This base is often finished with a layer of fine cement.

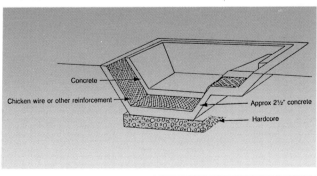

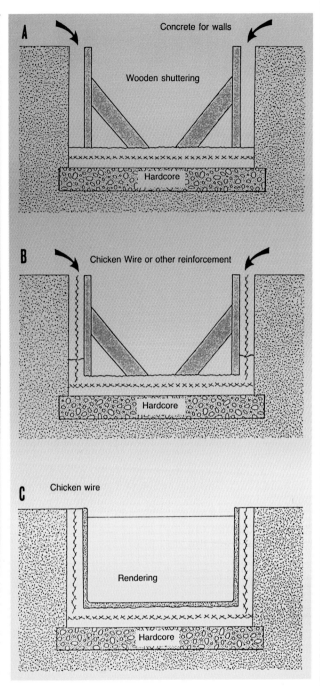

To construct the concrete sides of a pond, it is wise to use wooden shuttering so as to allow the concrete to set.

(A) The shuttering should leave at least a six-inch gap between itself and the earth wall.

(B) Slowly pour the concrete and insert chicken wire or other suitable reinforcement material.

(C) Apply the rendering, leaving no awkward ridges or depressions; create the smoothest finish you can.

Step 8 FORMAL PONDS ONLY—Install shuttering if the pond is small enough to allow this to be done without having to step on the wet concrete. If the pond is too large for this, allow the base to dry out for about one day before installing the shuttering.

NOTE: *Though it is possible to lay the walls down in two stages (as the base), this can prove quite complicated and involves two shuttering operations. It is far easier to arrange the shuttering so it will allow you to construct vertical walls 5 in (12 cm) thick in a single operation.*

Step 9 FORMAL PONDS ONLY—Mix up concrete of the same grade and consistency as that used for the pond base and shovel this into the cavity between the shuttering and the excavation walls, having first wetted the shuttering with soapy water or limewash to prevent the concrete sticking to it. Make sure that no air-traps are created.

Reinforcing chicken wire, mesh or rods can be installed quite easily once there is a layer of wet concrete several centimeters deep at the base of each cavity. These reinforcements can be prevented from collapsing or being forced out of position by providing appropriate temporary supports along the top edge of the shuttering/excavation cavity and by filling in carefully. Keep the levels of concrete equal outside and inside the reinforcing structures.

Step 10 FORMAL PONDS ONLY—Allow the sides to set for one day.

Step 11 FORMAL PONDS ONLY—Remove shuttering.

Step 12 FORMAL PONDS ONLY—Complete laying pond base if it was left incomplete at end of **Step 7.** The final thickness should be around 5 in (12 cm.)

Step 13 FORMAL PONDS ONLY—Allow final base layer to dry out for one day.

Step 14 FORMAL AND INFORMAL PONDS— Prepare a dry mixture consisting of 3 parts sharp sand : 1 part cement. Add waterproofing powder at this stage, if you wish to incorporate this into your mixture, following the manufacturer's instructions. If a colored finish is required, then the necessary pigments (available in powder form from building suppliers) should also be added to the mixture at this stage.

Step 15 Gently add water to the dry mixture until it has the consistency of a stiff paste. Ensure that you prepare enough of this final mixture (rendering) to cover the whole of the pond surface to about 1 in (2.5 cm) in one continuous operation.

Step 16 Apply the rendering with a trowel or other suitable tool, leaving no awkward ridges or depressions. Create the smoothest finish you can. Work as quickly as possible, turning over the stock mixture from time to time to prevent it from drying out.

Step 17 You may find that a small amount of water may collect at the bottom of the pond. If this happens, it should disappear within an hour or so. If the weather is hot, many of the surfaces will begin to lose their wet look even before this. If so, cover all these drying surfaces with moist sacking to slow down the drying out process, since excessively fast drying leads to cracks and a soft, flaky surface.

Step 18 Opinions vary as to how long one should wait before adding water to the pond. If the weather is damp but not cold, one can safely allow the cement to dry out completely over a period of a week or so. On the other hand, if the weather is very dry, the pond can be filled with water after 2 days without any serious risks.

HOW TO MAKE A CEMENT POND SAFE FOR STOCKING

A newly-constructed, newly-filled concrete pond may look safe, but appearances can be deceiving. It is far too raw and hostile to all forms of life, so it must be made safe before any fish or plants are introduced.

The main danger comes from lime, an essential component of cement, which is also a killer, even when present in small quantities. Therefore one cannot afford to be in a desperate hurry when it comes to stocking cement-based ponds. This is one of the main reasons why it

A newly constructed, freshly filled concrete pond may look safe, but in fact it is not. Consult your local pet store owner for ideas concerning pond maturation and for products that help tomake "raw" water safer for fishes. Preparations for de-chlorinating water are sold by petshops, for example, in both pond-size, and aquarium-size units.

makes good sense to build such a pond in the autumn. If need be, one can dedicate the whole of the winter to achieving a safe level of pond maturity, which will be appreciated by fish and plants alike the following spring. Things can be speeded up considerably, though, by sealing the pond in one way or other. The whole process of priming, sealing, and curing can be carried out in as little as two weeks or so by using well-known, easily available sealing agents. Two of the basic requirements with many sealers are priming the raw, dry cement properly beforehand and allowing each coat of sealer to dry out before the

next one is applied. After the final coat, a longer drying out period of up to two weeks (depending on weather conditions) will ensure complete chemical resistance, preventing any leaching out of lime.

There is now a polyurethane resin which can cut back this waiting period to just three days, with only 30-45 minutes being required between coats. In fact, this material can be applied straight on to cement, stone or most other surfaces without prior priming.

It is important to remember with all sealing agents that they can only be expected to work if complete coats are applied. No hole, however small, must be left unpainted. Failing this, lime will, obviously, leach out.

Once a pond has been sealed, it needs to be filled and drained several times to rinse out any impurities and render it safe. With the polyurethane sealer mentioned above, a wash with a gentle detergent, followed by a rinse and a refill, is deemed sufficient. Though using a sealing agent cuts down the waiting period dramatically (something that is an even greater advantage during the warmer, drier months), it is quite feasible to establish a safe pond without using any sealer at all. The one essential requirement is patience. Numerous refills at roughly weekly intervals will be needed for up to two months. Once more, autumn is the ideal time for this.

One final point on the subject: priming and sealing should, obviously, be delayed until the pond edging has been completed if cement or concrete is being used during this stage of construction.

A concrete pond may take a little more time to become safe for plants and animals, but, once the pond is fully mature, it should provide a lifetime of enjoyment, as such ponds are extremely durable and resistant to the wear and tear of use and weather.

CHECKLIST FOR INSTALLING CONCRETE PONDS

Step 1 Excavate pond following general principles described for lined ponds, but allow for:
- 6 in (15 cm) layer of hardcore
- 6 in (15 cm) base
- 4 in (10 cm) sloping sides
- 6 in (15 cm) vertical sides

Step 2 Lay compacted hardcore to depth of 6 in (15 cm.)

Step 3 Prepare dry concrete mixture.

Step 4 Add water to achieve working consistency.

Step 5 SMALL INFORMAL PONDS—Lay bottom and sides to depth of 5 in (12 cm.)

Step 5 LARGE INFORMAL PONDS—Lay bottom to depth of around 2¼ in (6 cm.)

Step 5 SMALL FORMAL PONDS–Lay bottom to depth of 5 in (12 cm) if shuttering can be installed immediately. If shuttering cannot be installed, part-lay bottom and key it.

Step 5 LARGE FORMAL PONDS—Lay bottom to depth of 5 in (6 cm.)

Step 6 INFORMAL PONDS—Put reinforcing wire/mesh in position along base and sides.

Step 6 FORMAL PONDS—Restrict reinforcements to base.

Step 7 LARGE INFORMAL PONDS—Complete laying base to depth of 5 in (12 cm.) (Omit **Steps 8-12** and continue as from **Step 14.)**

Step 8 FORMAL PONDS—Install shuttering.

Step 9 Mix up concrete and start building up pond sides.

Step 10 Install side reinforcements and complete building up pond sides.

Step 11 Allow sides to set.

Step 12 Remove shuttering.

Step 13 Complete laying bottom if left unfinished at end of **Step 7**. Allow base to set.

Step 14 FORMAL AND INFORMAL PONDS— Prepare cement mixture. (Add waterproofing or coloring powder if so desired.)

Step 15 Add smooth 1 in (2.5 cm) layer of cement (rendering) to base and sides.

Step 16 Allow cement to dry slowly, covering with damp sacking if necessary.

Step 17 Fill pond with water (this can be done any time from one to seven days after completion.)

Step 18 Drain pond after a day and allow to dry out completely if sealing is desired, or drain and refill pond after a few days if sealing is not required or desired.

Step 19 Seal the pond surface with a proprietary mixture, or commence maturing process by periodic filling, draining and refilling of untreated pond.

BLOCK PONDS

Block ponds are so named because the sides are built of cinder blocks, cement blocks or bricks. The variety of these now available, and the versatility of the materials themselves, means that block ponds can be built to fit a wide range of tastes. Despite this, bricks and blocks are best suited for use on raised ponds of predominantly formal design.

Some advantages of raised block ponds (which apply equally to other types of raised ponds) are:
- There is no soil to dispose of.
- The fish are often easier to observe.
- People are inclined to sit on the surrounding wall, which minimizes the risk of anyone falling in.
- Because of the above, these ponds are among the most suitable for the very young and the elderly.
- If the walls are about 20 in (50 cm) high,

Despite the advantages of a concrete pond, if your desire is to own a wildlife pond, a concrete pond is probably not suited to your needs.

raised ponds are also the most suitable for wheelchair-bound pondkeepers.

CONSTRUCTING A BLOCK POND

Unlike sunken ponds, block ponds need only the minimum of digging—just enough to take the foundations and the concrete base. So this otherwise labor-intensive part of the job is easy, quick and relatively painless.

Step 1 Excavate a hole just slightly larger than the size of the pond base and about 12 in (30 cm) deep.

Step 2 Dig out a shallow trench about 2 in (5 cm) deep and 10 in (25 cm) wide around the perimeter of the base excavation. (The reason for this will become apparent later on.)

Step 3 Cover the base of the excavation with compacted hardcore (crumbled stones, or bricks) to a depth of about 6 in (15 cm) all round. (This should leave you with 2 in (5 cm) step down into trench.)

Step 4 Make up a 3:2:1 dry mixture of concrete from 3 parts coarse aggregate 2 parts sharp sand : 1 part cement. Mix thoroughly.

Step 5 Add sufficient water to achieve a consistency that will allow a slit made with the spade to remain open, or ridges to maintain their shape.

Step 6 Lay a concrete base measuring about 2½ in (6 cm) over the pond bottom and 4½ in (11 cm) over the perimeter trench.

Step 7 Cover this layer with heavy gauge chicken wire to provide extra base strength if necessary. As with concrete ponds, reinforcing steel mesh or rods can be used instead. Ensure that the reinforcing structures are bedded into the wet concrete.

Step 8 Lay the remaining concrete to a maximum depth of 5 in (12 cm.) This will give you a thickness of about 7 in (17 cm) over the perimeter trench which will provide the foundation for the block wall later on.

Step 9 Allow the concrete to set and dry for a day.

Step 10 Soak the bricks or blocks in water. They will then 'accept' cement more easily.

Step 11 Prepare a 3:1 dry mixture of 3 parts sharp sand : 1 part cement. Mix thoroughly.

Step 12 Add sufficient water to achieve the consistency of a stiff paste.

Step 13 Lay the first row of bricks or blocks right around the pond, checking your levels as you go. Every once in a while (but at regular intervals), lay a brick at right angles to the general trend to

A do-it-yourself pebble fountain base and surround can be quite easily constructed from bricks and cement.

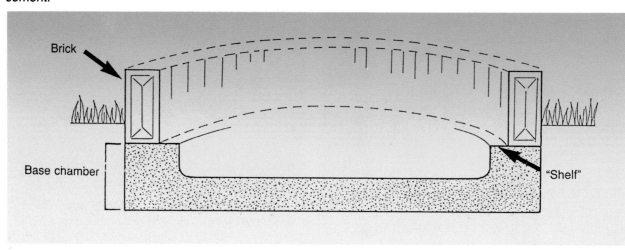

Brick

Base chamber

"Shelf"

form a strengthening strut between this row and the second, referred to in **Step 14.**

Step 14 Repeat **Step 13** to give you a double first row of bricks, leaving a gap of around just under 1 in (2 cm) between the outer and inner rows. Check levels frequently.

Step 15 Continue as above until the wall is completed.

Step 16 Allow to set for a day.

Step 17 If wall reinforcement is desired, insert chicken wire or steel rods vertically into the gap between the inner and outer walls and fill the gap with cement made up as in **Steps 11** and **12.** Considerable strength can also be provided by just filling the gap with cement and omitting the wire/rod reinforcement altogether.

Step 18 Add the final coat (rendering) using exactly the same method as with concrete ponds (see **Steps 14-16.)**

Step 19 Safe drying out of the rendering is carried out as outlined for concrete ponds (see **Steps 17** and **18.)**

Step 20 A newly-constructed block pond is as raw and unsafe as a newly-constructed concrete one.

The pressure exerted by water can be great. Your block wall should be at least two blocks thick. Reinforcement can be added between these blocks.

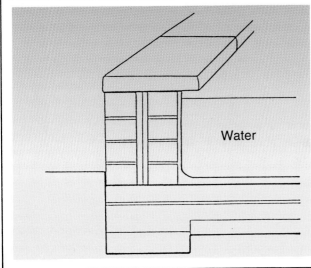

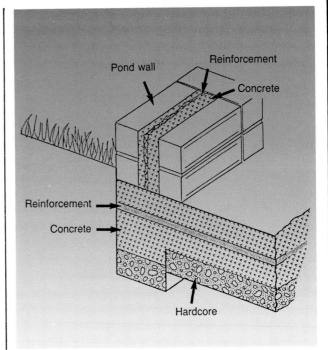

As with the concrete pond, the block pond is composed of layers of concrete, reinforcement, and of course blocks. As with the concrete pond, the base of the block pond rests on a layer of level, compressed hardcore.

Checklist of Steps Involved in Installing Block Ponds

1. Excavate base and trench, making allowances for:
   a) 6 in (15 cm) hardcore.
   b) 6 in (15 cm) base.
   c) 7 in (17 cm) thickened base for walls.
2. Lay compacted hardcore to depth of 6 in (15 cm.)
3. Prepare dry concrete mixture.
4. Add water to achieve working consistency.
5. Lay base to depth of about 2½ in (6 cm) over pond bottom and 4½ in (11 cm) over trench.
6. Install base reinforcements if necessary.
7. Complete laying concrete to final depth of 5 in (12 cm) over pond bottom and 7 in (17 cm) over trench.
8. Allow concrete to dry.
9. Soak bricks/blocks in water.
10. Prepare dry cement mixture.
11. Add water to achieve working consistency.

In terms of location, sink and tub ponds are so versatile as to fit almost anywhere. In terms of suitability for most wildlife, however, most sink and tubs ponds are simply too small to safely house many species of plants and fish.

12. Lay first double row of bricks leaving small gap between inner and outer walls and installing regular front/back 'brick struts'. Check levels regularly.
13. Repeat **Step 12** until wall is completed.
14. Allow cement to set.
15. Add reinforcing wire/rods and/or cement in gap between inner and outer walls.
16. Prepare final coat (rendering) of cement, including waterproofing and/or coloring powder if so wished.
17. Apply 1 in (2.5 cm) smooth coat of rendering to base and walls.
18. Allow rendering to dry slowly, covering it with damp sacking if necessary.
19. Fill pond with water (any time between 1 and 7 days after completion.)
20. a) Drain pond after a day and allow to dry out completely if sealing is desired; or
    b) Drain and refill after several days if sealing is not going to be carried out.
21. a) Seal pond surface with proprietary preparation; or
    b) Commence maturation process of periodic fillings, drainings and refillings if pond is to remain untreated.

SINK AND TUB PONDS

Virtually any container that will hold water and is made of a non-toxic material, or one that can be made safe, can be used as a miniature pond. The two most commonly encountered are ceramic sinks and wooden half-barrels. The small size of these water features makes them ideal for the smallest patios, where a little creative flair can bring a living, brilliant splash of color to the most drab of surroundings during late spring, summer and early autumn.

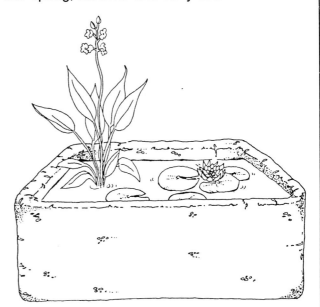

Sink and tub ponds can be made using already existing pots and tubs, or they can be created by using brick, concrete, or other suitable material.

However, small size can have a number of disadvantages. The selection of plants and fish suitable for such containers is relatively restricted compared with a full-sized pond. Small containers are also quite unsuitable as overwintering quarters for most fish and quite a few plants. Therefore, an important aspect to consider is the provision of alternative winter accommodation (in an aquarium or full-sized pond for the chosen inhabitants.) The most sensible solution, if you cannot provide this, is simply to pass your stocks on to a friend who can, when temperatures begin to drop in the autumn. As always, the welfare of fish and plants must be given top priority.

The stepping stones illustrated here are actually barrels that have been covered with a bonding agent to make them water-tight. With the addition of a stonelike finish, these barrels have been made an attractive focal point of the pond.

SINK PONDS

Any glazed ceramic sink can be used for this type of pond. Old ones can be picked up for next to nothing. On the other hand, since new sinks are quite expensive, there seems little point in choosing one of these. It is, perhaps, more sensible to go for a different type of small water feature if a second-hand sink is not available.

Step 1 Clean the sink thoroughly, inside and out. Avoid using detergent or, if you do, rinse thoroughly.

Step 2 Seal the plug hole and the overflow. This can be done in various ways, e.g. the plug itself can be sealed in, using one of the proprietary silicone-based aquarium sealants.

Step 3 Allow sealant to cure for a day or so.

Step 4 Spread an even coat of a bonding agent on all the exposed surfaces. Some of the proprietary 'tacky' glues used for bonding formica sheets are quite suitable for this.

Step 5 Make up two dry mixtures. 3 parts sand : 1 part cement and 2 parts peat : 1 part sand : 1 part cement.

Step 6 Add sufficient water to the sand/cement mixture to obtain a stiff but workable consistency.

Step 7 When the bonding agent becomes tacky (usually within minutes), apply an even coat of moist sand/cement mixture to the base and inside walls of the sink. Aim at a layer ½ to 1 in (1.2 to 2.5 cm) thick. Extend the coating on the sides to within 1 in (2.5 cm) of the rim.

Step 8 Add sufficient water to the peat/sand/cement mixture to obtain a stiff, but workable consistency.

Step 9 Apply a coat of the moist peat/sand/cement mixture to the outside walls of the sink, extending the layer over the rim and down the top edge of the inside walls to overlap the sand/cement coat laid earlier. Wear rubber gloves for this stage and work the peat/sand/cement mixture with your hands to create an uneven, stonelike finish. The peat will produce a natural rock-like effect when the mixture dries, hiding the otherwise artificial look of raw cement.

Step 10 Allow the cement to dry out, covering it with moist sacking if the weather is hot and dry.

Step 11 Fill the pond with water any time within one and seven days after completion.

Step 12 Follow sealing and maturing steps described for concrete and block ponds.

TUB PONDS

Most wooden vinegar, wine, sherry, or spirit barrels are quite suitable for tub ponds if cut in half. Unsuitable barrels for this type of pond are those used for oil-based, or other toxic chemicals. New or cured half-barrels are ideal and can be obtained through many aquatic and gardening outlets. Tub ponds can be used either free-standing on a flat, solid base, or sunken (dug into the ground so that the rim is level with the surroundings.)

In the latter case, the iron supporting rings will rust away in time but the inward pressure of the soil will counteract the outward pressure of the water in the pond, so no problems should arise. One clear advantage of a sunken pond is that it minimizes the temperature fluctuation to which all small raised ponds are susceptible.

RAISED TUB PONDS

Step 1 Scrub the inside of the barrel thoroughly. Use warm water if desired, but avoid the use of detergents. Rinse several times.

Step 2 Allow barrel to dry out thoroughly.

Step 3 Waterproof the inside with bitumen (roofing) paint or other suitable waterproofing agent if necessary. (Bought tub ponds may not require this treatment.

Step 4 Allow waterproofing coat to dry out completely.

Step 5 Fill the pond and leave it for a few days.

Step 6 Drain and refill several times before use.

The specifics of many aspects of garden pond construction are not independent entities, for many of the ideas concerning one type of pond can be adapted to any other type. For example, the island construction witnessed here was constructed by using barrels coated with a water-tight bonding agent and given a stonelike finish (as per Step 9, Sink Ponds).

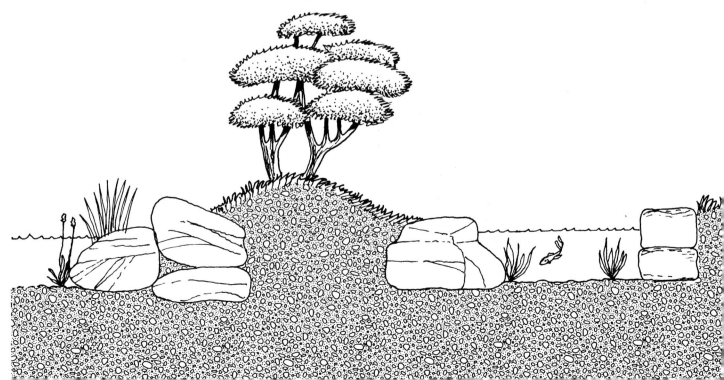

SUNKEN TUB PONDS

Follow the instructions outlined above for raised tub ponds; then:

Step 1 Dig a hole several inches larger and deeper than the tub pond.

Step 2 Cover the bottom of the hole with a layer of compacted sand and work the base of the tub pond firmly into position.

Step 3 Check that the rim of the tub is flush with the surroundings and perfectly level.

Step 4 Fill the 'circumference' gap between the tub and the excavation with sand. Compact it as you go along to provide even support all around. (This support will become vital later when the tub's iron reinforcements rust away.)

Small sunken ponds can be made exquisite by the addition of a spray or other fountain. The spray fountain can be ideal for moisture-loving plants, as it will increase the humidity of the immediately surrounding air. The biggest drawback of sunken ponds is their smallness in size, as smaller ponds tend not to be suitable for most species of fish, especially if they are located in colder climates.

6
Pebble Fountains and Other Water Features

There can be few sounds more soothing than that of moving water. As far as ponds are concerned, this can be provided quite easily by incorporating fountains and/or water courses into the design. If you do not have the space (or inclination) for a sizeable patio or garden pond, you can still accommodate a moving-water feature, and it need not take up a great deal of space either.

By far the simplest way of doing this is to buy one of the manufactured kits now available, such as millstone fountains, from your local petshop. These kits are easy to assemble and can provide an attractive water feature in next to no time. If you prefer the do-it-yourself approach, you can construct a similar feature, e.g. a pebble fountain, to meet your exact needs. All these decorative systems have several things in common:

1. They are small.
2. They provide attractive moving water displays.
3. They are not intended to accommodate fish or plants (though it is possible to include certain spray-loving plants in some designs.)
4. They all have a small base reservoir.
5. They require a pump to drive the water around.
6. They require regular topping up.

CONSTRUCTING A BASE CHAMBER

If you opt for a do-it-yourself design, you will need to construct a base chamber. There are various ways of doing this, the following being just one.

Step 1 Dig a circular trench of the required diameter. The depth (just like the diameter) is entirely up to you, but do bear in mind that if you make it too big, you are likely to end up with a mini-pond rather than a pebble fountain. A depth of around 6-8 in (15-20 cm) is perfectly adequate. If the diameter is too big, much of the visual effect will be lost (something around 3 ft (1 m) should prove quite suitable.)

Step 2 Lay a base of cement or concrete measuring about 3 in (7 cm) thick. (See concrete ponds for details of cement mixture.)

Step 3 Slope up the cement around the edges to give a wide lip all round, at least wider than a brick. (See **Step 5** for explanation.)

Step 4 Allow the base and lip to set for about one day.

Step 5 Build a low brick wall to fit around the

Fountains come in a wide variety of shapes and sizes; they therefore can be included in almost any garden pond. Visit your local pet store to get an idea of the full range of available fountains and other water features.

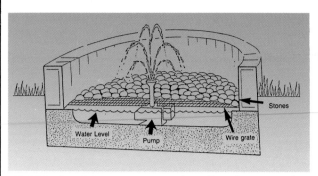

Pebble fountains are easy to install and are usually small enough to be placed anywhere.

outside edge of the lip. You can lay the bricks in an upright position (in which case, a single row will suffice), or in their more usual horizontal position (when you will probably need two rows.) Since the lip is considerably wider than a brick, you should end up with an internal shelf all the way around the circular trough.

Step 6 Allow the wall to dry out thoroughly.

Step 7 Scrub the trough and wall with clean water and rinse out thoroughly.

Step 8 Lay a few supporting rods on the shelf to form a framework across the trough at 'lip' level. Stainless steel or other strong rustproof materials should be used for this.

Step 9 Cut out a circular sheet of strong plastic-coated mesh (or other suitable rust-proof material.) The diameter of the piece of mesh should be just slightly smaller than that of the internal shelf.

Step 10 Cut out a central hole in the circular sheet of mesh.

Step 11 Place the selected pump in the center of the trough.

Step 12 Lay the circular sheet of mesh on top of the supporting framework constructed in **Step 8**, fitting the central hole over the pump outlet piece.

Step 13 Cover the mesh with a layer of washed, rounded pebbles, making sure that the outlet pipe is hidden from view while the outlet itself remains unobstructed.

Step 14 Fill the trough with water, completely covering the pump (if it is of the submersible type) but ensuring that the level of water does not go above the pebble layer.

Step 15 Once safe electrical connections have been carried out, the system is ready for use.

POINTS TO NOTE

One point worth re-emphasizing at this stage is that the main attraction of these systems (besides their small size) is the effect created by moving/splashing water. Inevitably, this will lead to considerable water loss through evaporation and wind action, so check the water level in the trough regularly (e.g. when you switch off the pump each night.) If the pump becomes exposed at any time, overheating and/or irreparable damage can result.

The type of outlet used in pebble fountains is a matter of personal choice, but mushroom and spray-type fountain fittings are particularly suitable for this type of water feature.

It is quite possible to add a central hollow raised stem to a pebble fountain. This can be made of simulated stone, e.g. fiberglass or other suitable material, such as light rocks cemented together to form a tower. The outlet from the pump is then fitted up the central cavity and the water is allowed to spray out at the top in a normal fountain display, or allowed to cascade down the column on to the pebbles below.

Another modification or refinement is the introduction of plain or colored lighting. Waterproof lighting units are available from several suppliers and can be used with spectacular results in pebble/millstone arrangements.

The construction method described in the step-by-step guide outlined above will result in a permanent pebble fountain (sunken cement trough.) If a movable design is required, this can be obtained by building the trough inside a wooden mold. If you opt for this approach, wet the inside of the mold with soapy water or limewash to prevent the cement from sticking to the wood. 'Movable/portable' are relative terms—cement remains heavy whatever the label.

7

Designing the Pond Edge

Though I have repeatedly stressed that the well-being of plants, fish and other aquatic organisms must rank as the most important consideration when designing a pond, the quality of the areas immediately around the water's edge also warrant close attention. They may not have any direct influence on the state of health of the pond inhabitants, but they do determine whether your pond will look just like a water-filled hole in the ground or an object of great beauty.

Two factors about the nature of pond edging which are well worth bearing in mind before you go out and buy any materials are that it must be compatible with the type of pond and it must be safe.

COMPATIBLE EDGING

If your pond is of formal design, surrounding it with an informal edging of irregularly shaped blocks of natural stone with plants growing between the cracks or trailing down to the water's edge is not the best option. Not only will the pond's regular shape (which is what gives it much of its appeal) be obscured, but the two contrasting styles will look totally mismatched.

Formal ponds are shown off to best advantage by an edging of regular shaped slabs laid in an orderly fashion.

Informal ponds, for their part, look quite wrong if surrounded by formal edging. However, the type of arrangement outlined in the first paragraph is ideal.

Intermediate arrangements are, of course, quite possible, particularly since many ponds are neither formal nor informal.

As far as wildlife ponds are concerned, nothing could look more incongruous than a paved edge. In fact, wildlife ponds look most natural when grass is allowed to grow down the edge of the water and this is combined with a considered planting of waterside/bog plants, such as Water Forget-me-not *(Myosotis palustris),* Bugle *(Ajuga reptans),* Rushes of various species, Creeping Jenny *(Lysimachia nummularia)* and other similar

The range of choices for the edging of your pond is almost as wide as the range of shapes for the pond itself. The materials used can be concrete, stone, brick, soil, tile, or almost any other suitable medium. The idea to keep in mind is that the edging should be compatible with the pond type and the surrounding environment of the pond.

Colored tile or painted concrete blocks can visually enhance a formal pond.

moisture-loving species. At a few spots around the edge, large, flattish, natural rocks can be worked into place to provide firm, safe, dry, viewing points.

SAFE EDGING

People seem to have an irresistible urge to come as close to the edge of a pond as possible. Some even have an incredible knack for falling in, despite your best precautions. In view of this, pond edges must be made as safe as possible, while remaining compatible.

Comfortable wide slabs (overlapping the wall on both sides and cemented firmly into position) are ideal for raised ponds, whether of concrete, block or prefabricated type. This kind of edging does not have to extend all the way around the pond. If a few slabs are missed out, the cavity can be filled with soil and attractively planted to complement the overall design.

As for sunken ponds (again, irrespective of type), the slabs or stones used should overlap the edge by about 2 in (5 cm.) This should be sufficient to hide the concrete/prefab/lined edge of the pond from view.

There are three main safety factors to consider when installing edging around sunken ponds:
1. The slabs or stones used should be wide enough to support a person safely, i.e. without toppling into the pond, even if the person concerned stands with his/her whole body weight directly over the 2 in (5 cm) overlap.
2. The anchored part of the slab or stones should rest on a firm, solid base (details of how to construct such a base, if necessary, can be found in the earlier section, **Excavating a lined pond**.
3. The slabs/stones must not have a slippery surface. Polished stones, like some of those used for crazy paving should not be used for pond edging. Even non-slippery stones can become covered in algae (or other types of slime), particularly in winter. If this happens, just give the affected areas a vigorous scrub with a stiff brush (do not use detergents!) The application of a solution of pond algicide afterwards should help discourage further growth.

BEDDING IN THE EDGING SLABS

Several bedding techniques can be used, each designed to meet a different need. Three such methods are outlined below.

BASIC METHOD EMPLOYING CEMENT: This is, perhaps, the simplest technique of all.

Step 1 Prepare a mixture consisting of 3 parts sand : 1 part cement.

Step 2 Add just enough water to achieve a working consistency.

Step 3 Apply a thin layer of cement directly on top of the lined/prefab/cement edge of the whole area that the slabs will take up.

Probably the most important consideration involved with making a pond edging is making sure that it is firmly imbedded.

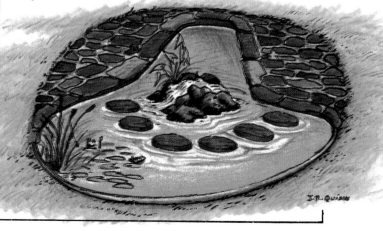

While the walls of the pond must be sturdy and strong, the edging need not be composed of rigid or permanent materials. The edging of your pond can be soil planted with an abundance of lush green plants. An edging of this type is very suitable to the informal and especially to the wildlife pond.

If the walls of your pond rise sufficiently above ground level, the edging can be of small pebbles or almost any other medium.

For this technique, a shallow, level shelf must be provided all the way round the pond. Although the normal 9 in (22 cm) pond shelf can be used, shallower shelves are better because they require fewer stacking blocks/slabs.

Because prefabricated and concrete ponds have rigid, sloping sides, this technique is most easily used on lined ponds.

Prefabricated Ponds Stability can be given to the stacked slabs by overlapping them backwards and cementing them together.

Concrete Ponds As the overlapping described above is being carried out, the gaps left under the slabs can be filled with cement to provide extra support.

Lined Ponds The inherent flexibility of liners does away with the need to employ either of the techniques just described. Instead, the slabs are stacked directly on a shelf, the liner is then wrapped virtually round the back and tucked in under the top slab to give a watertight finish. The stacked slabs and the top one could be cemented in for greater stability.

Stacking techniques hide lined/cement/prefab edges from view and give a pond a truly finished appearance. The fact that a liner is hidden from view also protects it from potentially harmful ultraviolet   rays. (Some liners become brittle after prolonged exposure to this type of radiation.)

On the debit side (besides the expense), stacking virtually eliminates any possibility of obtaining a gradual transition zone between pond and dry land.

Step 4 Bed the slabs in, checking that they are level and preventing any of the cement from dropping into the pond. If an excessive amount of cement does drop in, you will need to drain the pond if you have already started the maturation process described earlier.

Step 5 Allow the cement to dry for at least one day, preferably longer.

Alternative Method Employing Cement: Though the first method described is quite adequate for most ponds, it is possible to go a stage further with a little bit of extra effort (and at a little extra expense.) This second method is designed to ensure that the section of liner, plastic/fiberglass/polyester or cement between the water surface and the edging slabs is always hidden from view, even if evaporation causes the level of the water in the pond to drop significantly.

BEDDING METHOD AVOIDING THE USE OF CEMENT:

The non-cement technique is best reserved for informal and wildlife ponds. This method uses garden soil, preferably fine-grained, instead of cement, to bed in the edging slabs or stones.

One great advantage that soil has over any other material is that it provides a good rooting material for edging plants. With a little ingenuity, it is possible to create quite spectacular displays of waterside plants. The technique is simplicity itself.

Step 1 Spread a layer of soil directly on to the liner/cement/prefab edge of the pond.

Step 2 Select your plant and lay it on the soil with the roots directed away from the pond edge and towards the center of where the slab or stone is going to rest.

Step 3 Trail the stems and leaves over the pond edge (Use sufficient numbers of plants to cover up the liner/cement/prefab edging.)

Step 4 Cover up the roots with a liberal layer of soil.

Step 5 Bed in the slab on top of this second soil layer, taking care not to exert so much pressure that you damage the plants' roots.

Step 6 Repeat the process with a second slab or stone, leaving a gap (if desired) between it and the first slab or stone.

Step 7 Fill and plant the gap as outlined in **Steps 1** and **2** above.

POINTS TO NOTE

● The informality of this approach means that the slabs or stones of varying shapes and thicknesses can be used to great effect.
● Fine-grained soil is preferable because of its greater clay content. This will improve adhesion between the slabs or stones and the substratum as root growth expands and natural bedding-in occurs.

Be sure to include enough rooted plants to keep the surrounding earth from falling into the pond.

If the slabs are set firmly in soil then the grass is allowed to grow between them.

● Bedding-in and maximum adhesion take time to develop fully and can be helped along by keeping the soil moist. Autumn is, therefore, a good time for carrying out this type of pond edging.
● Even if the work is carried out in autumn and the slabs or stones bed-in properly, this technique cannot provide the sort of stability achieved with concrete bedding methods.
● Some loss of stability will also result if the soil is allowed to dry out during hot weather. Fortunately, the fact that the edging plants require water to survive should ensure that total drying out will not occur (at least, not too often.)
● Although the plants used have their roots close to water, they do not necessarily experience marshy or boggy conditions. In fact, most will be subjected to normal garden conditions or even, since relatively thin layers of soil are used, fluctuating wet/dry conditions. Both of these provide suitable environments for a wide range of plants, including species such as Houseleeks *(Sempervivum* spp) at the dry end of the spectrum and *Astilbes* and *Hostas* at the other. Plants as diverse as Creeping Jenny *(Lysimachia nummularia)*, Primroses *(Primula* spp), Creeping or Dwarf Thyme *(Thymus serpyllum)*, Cranesbill *(Geranium* sp), and even prostrate conifers, such as *Juniperus squamata* or *J. communis* 'Prostrata', can all be incorporated quite successfully into this type of pond edging scheme.

A little creative flair can go a long way in pond layout. The edging of this pond is of green plants growing in firm soil, with small trees and bushes to act as wind-breakers, and well spaced stone slabs to serve as a footpath. The fallen tree used as a footbridge adds a nice natural touch.

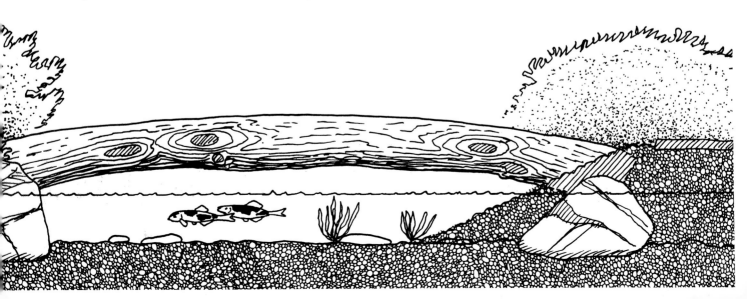

8

Fountains, Watercourses, Waterfalls, Cascades and Ornaments

With the exception of millstone and pebble fountains, all the water schemes that have been mentioned so far are still-water systems. To many water gardeners, this is precisely what a pond should be. Ponds are, after all, small, usually artificial, lakes. Though this is true, there is no logical reason why there should not be additions or embellishments to the basic design. In fact, some ponds, particularly formal ones, can look quite incomplete without at least one ornament placed somewhere around the edge (or in the water itself.) This could be a statue serving a purely decorative purpose, or one which combines decorative and functional qualities with a fountain or gushing stream of water.

FOUNTAINS

Away from the ornaments themselves, decorative/functional features can also be provided by fountain pumps which lie fully immersed at a strategic point in the pond (and, thus, hidden from view), with just the outlet pipe projecting slightly above the water surface. The design of outlets has come in for a great deal of experiment in recent years. It is now possible to create virtually any spray pattern desired, ranging from a mushroom-type design, to a single upright water stream, with every possible permutation in between.

In addition to their obvious esthetic value, these arrangements also perform some very useful functions. For a start, they create water movement which, in turn, helps to stabilize the temperature of the water throughout the pond. Secondly, water turbulence is about the most efficient method of aeration, and fountains are, obviously, ideally suited for this job.

Many aspects of pondkeeping rely heavily on personal opinion and the choice of an

appropriate fountain is no exception. Despite this, some guidelines can be offered to fountain selection.

High water sprays are more likely to be deformed by even light gusts of wind than lower ones, particularly if the individual water jets are not very powerful or robust. Small ponds, especially, tend to look unbalanced if they have a powerful fountain pump which spurts water up high.

Equally unsuitable arrangements are narrow or small ponds fitted with wide-spraying fountains. The opposite applies to larger ponds.

Most pond owners and water gardeners will sooner or later opt for some water movement in their design, so it is of the utmost importance that the right decision be made at the outset.

Not only is it important to match fountain and pond as outlined above. It is equally relevant to

Pond kits, both large and small, for both large and small ponds, are available at your local pet store, as are many other pond accessories.

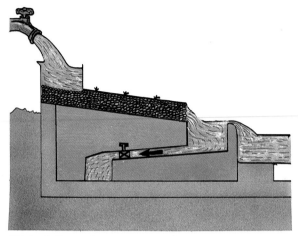

Waterfalls, watercourses and cascades invariably will require the installation of a pump system. The arrow marks the intake valve, while the spigot at top left is the outlet.

consider how compatible your envisaged choice is with your existing pond. How, for example, could you have a wildlife pond with such an obviously artificial feature as a fountain and still call it a wildlife pond? However, a spring or bubbling brook design involving the use of a pump arrangement like that found in millstone and pebble fountains, can produce an attractive display. It is also a functional one enjoyed by birds, insects and pond owner alike.

WATERFALLS, WATERCOURSES AND CASCADES

A similarly appropriate choice would consist of a waterfall, watercourse or cascade. All these features are very adaptable and can be used, with appropriate modification, in most water schemes.

In wildlife and informal ponds, waterfalls, courses and cascades should consist of prefabricated or home-built units which avoid straight-walled channels. Such a wide range of these is now available from water garden centers and other specialist outlets that there seems to be a strong case for avoiding the do-it-yourself approach altogether.

While it may still be true to say that some of the cheaper versions are somewhat flimsy and look too artificial—not rock-like—the better end of the market is now represented by molded designs made out of reconstituted stone or other suitable alternatives that look remarkably authentic, particularly when they begin to weather and adopt a veneer of mosses and other moisture-loving, encrusting plants.

Waterfalls, courses and cascades, like fountains, help to circulate and oxygenate the pond water and make it safe for fish.

There are few things in nature more beautiful and more awe inspiring than waterfalls. With all the available pumps, rock-work, and other accessories available, it seems inconceivable to some not to add a waterfall to their water garden.

This diagram shows the flow of water created by a well constructed waterfall and fountain. The circulation of water as shown is beneficial to most fish and other pond animals.

Waterfalls, courses and cascades for formal ponds do not necessarily have to have straight edges, though these are the most popular and can look very effective. Nowadays, there are all sorts of formal-looking, attractive units, such as kidney-shaped, lipped troughs which can be installed individually to act as a header pool with a single outflow into the pond, or as an impressive multiple-unit cascade.

Most of these waterfalls, courses and cascades can be obtained in water garden centers and other 'aquatic' businesses, while some of the more unusual ones are also available via landscaping outlets.

ESSENTIAL COMPONENTS OF A WATERFALL, WATERCOURSE OR CASCADE SYSTEM

When installing or constructing waterfalls, watercourses or cascades, one must not forget that their greatest tangible asset (besides looking good) is that splashing water makes a very pleasant, soothing sound. It also aids aeration, but this is not usually foremost in people's minds when they decide to install one of these systems.

From the pond inhabitants' point of view, of course, it doesn't matter in the least whether the design constitutes an eyesore or not. As long as they receive an adequate supply of oxygen, they will be happy. Incidentally, the same applies to water turbulence in ponds as in aquaria. In the latter, aeration is always linked, not just with oxygenation, but with the removal of excess carbon dioxide from the water through diffusion. Since the situation in ponds is no different in physical-chemical terms, it follows that surface turbulence, by whatever means, will result in the elimination of potentially toxic carbon dioxide and other harmful gases at the same time as oxygen diffuses in.

Applying this in practice to the installation of falls and other similar features, it becomes obvious that they will only be of any real use if they make provision for water to splash from a higher level to a lower one.

This is usually achieved by means of a lip or sill built on to the front edge of the individual units. If you buy a ready-made system, this sill will almost certainly be of an appropriate width. This apparently minor detail is very important, because if the sill is too wide, water will simply trickle over the edge rather than rush through and splash on to the unit below at anything like a decent rate.

If you are thinking about building your own units (applying the same basic techniques described for concrete ponds earlier), don't be tempted by visions of wide, gushing waterfalls. Get things into perspective. Even if you could *construct* a wide, gushing waterfall, its value, in most garden ponds (which are hardly, if ever, the size of a real lake) would be debatable. Yet, a churning torrent will wreak havoc with anything you put in your pond, including most fish. Then, of course, pumps capable of producing this kind of effect are not cheap!

At the bottom of this photo we see the end of a water-course that is feeding into the pond. If thoughtfully planned, a waterfall, watercourse, or water cascade does not take away from a fountain; rather, the two will complement one another.

In general terms, the width of the sill should be around 6 in (15 cm) or less. At the other extreme, an excessively narrow sill will produce a jet of water rather than a curtain and should therefore be avoided. Again, in general terms, a pump capable of circulating water at the rate of the pond's capacity per hour, will produce a satisfactory waterfall, provided the sills are of a reasonable width.

To put this into figures, a pump servicing a 1900-liter (500 Imp. gal) pond should be able to turn over about 1900 liters (500 Imp. gal) of water per hour if it is to produce a decent waterfall.

Besides aerating the water via fountains or waterfalls, pumps can be used to drive pond water through a filter thus helping to provide clean water, along with all the other facilities already mentioned.

One important fact to bear in mind when installing a filter in line with any of the systems described above, is that the resistance provided by the filtering media will tend to slow down the overall flow of water. It is therefore a good idea to seek advice from a reputable pet dealer who will match pump, filter and water flow to your personal needs.

I referred earlier in the book to the large quantities of soil that even modest-sized excavations will produce. I also said that this soil could be used in landscaping around the pond. Watercourses, waterfalls and cascades, by definition, require elevated ground and can therefore prove perfect outlets for all this surplus soil. Surprisingly, quite a few people go wrong in this part of the overall pond scheme. Several potential pitfalls therefore deserve brief discussion.

A difference in levels is obviously essential between the point at which the water emerges from the pump outflow pipe and that at which it flows back into the pond. This will generally take the form of one or more uninterrupted sloping channels in the case of watercourses, a single main step if it is a waterfall, and a series of steps with a cascade.

Besides providing the water gardener with fish and plants, pet stores carry a wide range of supplies and accessories to make your water garden complete.

POTENTIAL PITFALLS

Steep slopes If the slope is too steep, a watercourse will become a torrent with few soothing qualities about it. The torrent will gush into the pond, creating unnecessary and undesirable water currents which would ceaselessly churn up any mulm or debris that would otherwise settle on the pond bottom. It is virtually impossible to obtain clear water in these conditions.

Waterfall Drops When it comes to waterfalls, it does not follow that the bigger the drop, the more impressive the water curtain will be. In fact, unless a very powerful pump is used, the broad stream of water that emerges from the waterfall sill will tend to 'join up' into a progressively narrower stream as the distance between the sill and the pond increases. The stream will also tend to be drawn backward towards the face of the fall, rather than drop perpendicularly into the pond, as it should. So what started off in the imagination as a fantastic waterfall could turn out to be no more than a wet, dripping wall.

When it comes to waterfalls, it does not follow that the bigger the drop, the better is the waterfall; it is much better to follow the idea presented in this artwork and to create a series of waterfalls as opposed to one large water drop.

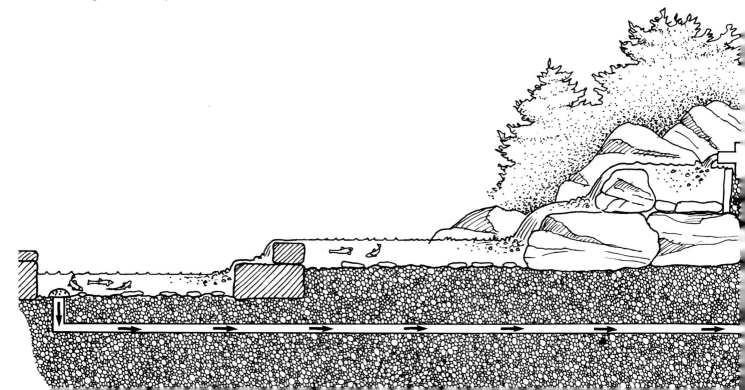

If the location of your pond is on sloping ground, an outstanding idea is to create several ponds at various levels, each flowing into the other. The use of a strong pump will be required to send the water back to the highest pond.

Rockeries One thing to be avoided at all costs is a rockery or pond surround that looks like an unattractive artificial steep pile of soil. Instead, one should aim to construct a rockery which looks as natural and pleasing to the eye as possible. This usually means one of modest height and gentle contours. Besides looking unsightly, high mounds require greater effort and expense to make them suitable for water-courses, falls or cascades. The number of units needed could be larger than for lower, gentler, sloping schemes and the pump needs to be more powerful and, hence, more expensive.

Siting the Inflow Pipe So far, I have referred to the water which flows out of a pump and into the pond. The other equally important half of this is the water that is taken out of the pond and pumped into the circulating system.

Opinions vary about the ideal siting of the inflow pipe and, in the end, personal preference could play a part. Some argue that placing the inflow pipe as far as possible from the return point creates a circular current of water which can affect some plants and fish adversely. This is likely either where the turnover rate is fast, or the pond is quite shallow. In deeper, larger ponds with a slower turnover rate, the effects could be minimal.

One way to avoid the problem is to site the inflow pipe as close to the return point as possible. On the credit side, siting the inflow close to the outflow cuts down the length of pipe or hose required. Since friction inside a hose will

If your pond is divided into sections, to perhaps separate aggressive fish, it may be a good idea to use a pump such as is used for waterfalls to better circulate the water between the divided sections.

Rockeries should not be constructed so steeply that appear artificial and thereby unattractive. The rockery presented in this photo has a nice, gradual slope, which gives it a natural and attractive appearance.

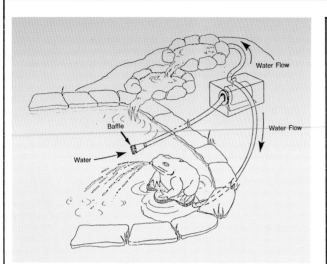

There are several opinions regarding the positioning of the inflow in relation to the outlet of a pump. If your fish or plants are sensitive to overly circulated water, it is best to site the inflow close to the outlet—as shown above.

slow down the flow of water, having the inlet and outlet close to each other exploits the efficiency of a pump better than the opposite arrangement.

A potential disadvantage of this technique is that it could leave some parts of the pond furthest from the inflow relatively undisturbed, or even partially stagnant. This applies especially to longish ponds with bends or shallow, densely planted sections, rather than to smaller, more open designs.

Combining Water Features Watercourses, falls and cascades generally look tremendous if they are planned well. But their effect can be virtually destroyed if they are installed in a pond designed to take a fountain as well. It could be that vertical and horizontal moving water do not go together visually, or that watercourses, falls and cascades are supposed to look natural, while fountains are meant to look artificial. Whatever the reason, many people find the vertical/horizontal combination does not look 'comfortable'. All the same, taste is a very personal thing. What others dislike intensely might well be just what you prefer. If so, nothing should stop you from going for the type of arrangement you like, provided your fish and plants do not suffer.

While it may be your preference to house a single water feature, such as the sole waterfall in the pond on the left, there is really no reason why several water features cannot be combined.

9
Pumps, Filters and Drains

Even the best drawn up plans of water schemes can go drastically wrong at the last minute by making the wrong decisions about the type and size of pump, filter or drain that is installed. I have already referred to all three subjects elsewhere in the book. In this chapter, I will deal with other aspects, such as various types of pumps, filters and drains that are available or can be constructed by the do-it-yourself enthusiast.

It must be said at the outset that perfectly adequate water schemes can be operated without a pump, filter or drain, as long as the basic rules of pondkeeping are adhered to. Of importance is siting the pond correctly, avoiding overstocking and overfeeding, having adequate surface cover and sufficient submerged oxygenating plants, etc.

Nonetheless, using these accessories can considerably extend a pond's scope. It can also make the job of establishing and maintaining favorable living conditions for its inhabitants significantly easier.

PUMPS

The range of pumps now available is quite staggering, and becoming ever more so with each new pondkeeping season. Still, pond pumps can be divided into two groups:

a) Surface (external) pumps.
b) Submersible (internal) pumps.

Surface or External Pumps As their name suggests, surface or external pumps are located outside the pond. They do the same job as submersible pumps, but they do it differently. On the credit side, many surface pumps are less expensive than equivalent submersible models. Being housed outside the pond allows checking, maintenance and repairs to be carried out without having to get one's hands wet. On the whole, external pumps are also more powerful than submersible ones. In fact, many are just too powerful for the average-sized garden or patio pond.

Your local pet store or garden pond supply center will have the pumps, filters and drains necessary to make your water garden a beautiful part of your lawn or garden. To acquire the ideal accessories for your needs, visit your local pet store.

On the debit side, surface pumps are easily damaged by moisture. I know this sounds illogical, but it is still true. Although water passes through the pump, the motor actually remains dry. What gets wet is the impellor which drives the water along the pipes from and to the pond. In fact, even prolonged damp conditions can adversely affect these pumps.

For this reason, surface pumps must be housed in dry, well-ventilated, waterproof chambers. As a further precaution, the pump itself should be raised slightly from the ground with wooden blocks or bricks.

The inlet tube is usually provided with a strainer to prevent debris entering the impellor chamber, where blockages can lead to overheating and permanent damage to the working parts. Since the impellor cannot suck in water (it merely moves it along), it follows that the impellor chamber must be primed before the pump can begin to operate. Priming simply involves filling the impellor chamber with water before switching the motor on. If the pump is located below pond level, the chamber can be filled under gravity. If, on the other hand, the pump is housed above the pond, water needs to be pumped into the chamber or poured into it via the outlet pipe.

The chamber can be prevented from emptying when the pump is not in use by means of a footvalve. Directions for all these operations are usually supplied with the pump, of course.

A surface pump should be housed quite close to the pond, but at a level that will allow it to suck in water. Again, details are supplied by manufacturers.

Submerged or Submersible Pumps Whereas surface pumps will be damaged if water gets into the motor, submersible pumps must be fully submerged before they are switched on. Although water will fill the chamber as soon as the pump is immersed in the pond, the 'electrics' are fully protected and therefore kept dry. As in surface models, the inlet pipe of a submersible pump usually carries a strainer or filter that will prevent debris from being sucked into the impellor chamber.

The effectiveness of the strainer can be gauged by how quickly the head of water produced by the pump diminishes. In very clean ponds, it may take a week or longer for a strainer to become clogged up, but in dirty conditions, small strainers may need to be cleaned out more often.

This rarely presents a problem. All you need to do is switch off the pump, remove the strainer (usually very simple), rinse it out under a running tap, and replace it. The whole job need take no more than a couple of minutes. The interval between clean-outs can be increased to an extent by resting the pump on bricks to keep it away from the mulm which inevitably accumulates on the pond bottom.

Submersible pumps have several advantages over surface models. They are out of sight, completely silent, easy to clean and require no priming. On the debit side, they are not usually as powerful as their surface equivalents. Powerful submersible pumps do exist, but they tend to be quite expensive.

Overall, while submersibles may be perfectly adequate for small and medium-sized water schemes, larger set-ups are probably better served by a surface pump. Some submersible models come with a single spray unit, while others can accommodate a range of sprays. Whichever you opt for, make certain that you install the pump in such a way that it exploits the spray to maximum effect. It is, of course, essential to rest the pump so that the tip of the spray unit is at right angles to the surface of the water. Few things look sorrier for themselves than an out-of-true fountain.

Most spray units are designed to be most effective when located just above water level, but mushroom-type fittings need to project some distance above the pond surface to produce their full effect.

FILTERS

Perfectly good, balanced ponds can be established without installing a filter. The key word here is 'balance' and, while the theory behind this notion is simple enough, its practical application is quite a different matter.

To many people, a balanced pond looks rather underpopulated. The temptation to add just a few more fish often proves too difficult to resist. Unfortunately, the margin of error between a balanced pond and an unbalanced one without a filter is narrower than one would think. Those few extra fish could well tip the scales irrevocably towards disaster. Clearly, the safest thing is to install some means of purifying the water to minimize the risks of overcrowding and allow you to accommodate those few extra fish safely.

A good filter is the obvious answer. Filters can perform a number of functions, from physically removing particles of debris, to chemically purifying the water or biologically eliminating toxic waste products such as ammonia and nitrites (both having deservedly formidable reputations as fish killers.)

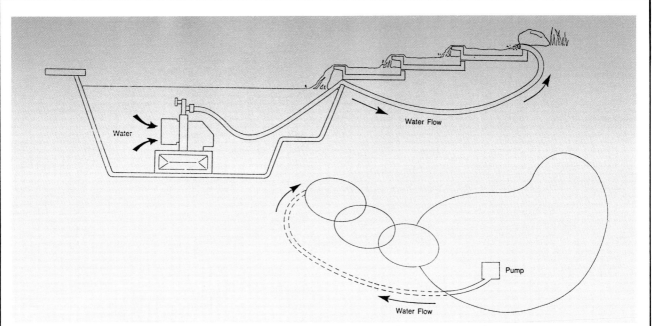

Pond pumps come in either of two types (external and submerged). Submerged pumps have the advantage of being located out of clear sight; indeed, the entire pump system in the above illustration is located out of sight.

Mechanical Filtration This type of filtration physically removes suspended particles of debris by passing the dirty water through gravel, clinker, filter floss, filter foam or other suitable physical barrier. The use of floss is largely restricted to aquaria; the others are widely used both in ponds and aquaria.

Chemical Filtration/Purification Toxic chemicals such as ammonia can be removed through absorption by passing contaminated water over a suitable medium. The two most common media used in aquaria are activated charcoal and zeolite (clay-based particles.) Chemical filtration methods were not often used in ponds, the job of purifying the water usually being done by biological means. Several new products have, however, recently come on the market combining mechanical and chemical filtration (purification is probably a better term) and are now widely used, especially in new ponds. Complete petshops or aquarium stores usually have new products for water purification.

Biological Filtration/Purification Though many bacteria produce diseases in plants and animals, some actually perform a beneficial role by breaking down toxic substances such as ammonia (produced as a waste product by

aquatic organisms) into nitrites. This is only part of the story, though, because nitrites, which are also toxic, are then converted into relatively harmless nitrates by other bacteria. Nitrates are only toxic if allowed to accumulate to comparatively high levels.

Fortunately, plants require nitrates for healthy growth, so well-filtered, well-planted ponds exploit the by-products of biological filtration (purification) to the full.

Though I have kept the three types of filtration/purification separate, I do not wish to imply that they are as mutually exclusive as this might indicate. In practice, most types of pond filter perform both mechanical filtration and biological purification. Further, since ammonia and nitrites are also eliminated (by digestive rather than absorptive means), we could say that most pond filters are capable of carrying out all three methods of filtration.

Mechanical filtration is effective from the moment a filter is switched on. Biological purification, on the other hand, takes several weeks, at comfortable temperatures, to start having a significant influence. In fact, several months may need to elapse before maximum biological capacity is established.

Whether this is achieved or not, and to what extent, will depend on several factors. If the pond

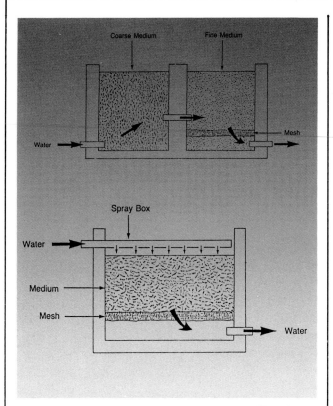

The above two drawings illustrate a pond filter that uses a coarse- and a fine-grain medium to perform both mechanical and biological filtration.

water is too acid, biological activity will be reduced. Neutral to slightly alkaline water seems to suit this type of 'metabolic' breakdown better. Such conditions can be encouraged by using alkaline materials, e.g. limestone or marble chips, as part of the filter medium.

Since biological purification depends on bacterial activity, it follows that any anti-bacterial disease treatment put into a pond will affect the beneficial bacteria as much as the pathogenic or disease-causing ones. This is, perhaps, the only significant disadvantage of this type of filter.

TYPES OF POND FILTER

Pond filters fall into two main categories: internal and external. Whether it performs purely a mechanical function or a mechanical/biological one depends more on how a filter is run than on its type.

If the pond is treated regularly with chemicals, then biological activity will be, at best, minimal. But if a filter is allowed to run for several weeks

without chemical treatment, it will inevitably develop a degree of biological activity. Therefore, when a filter needs to be cleaned, no cleaning agents, other than water, should be used. Dirt will then be removed without killing off the beneficial bacteria, and biological activity will be only temporarily slowed down.

Internal Filters: Perhaps the biggest advantage that internal filters have is that they are located under water and, consequently, out of sight. One of the biggest disadvantages of some types is that they cannot be readily serviced on a regular basis. Therefore, once such a filter is in, it is in for keeps.

To be really effective, a constructed (permanent) filter must have an overall surface area equal, at least, to about a third of the total pond surface area. It should also contain a layer of filtering medium, such as gravel, measuring at least 12 in (30 cm) thick. Clearly, if you are planning to install such a filter, you need to make allowances for it when you plan your excavation.

Generally, constructed internal filters are built to the same basic design which can be altered to suit individual circumstances.

One other point worth noting is that these internal filters are constructed, rather than installed, so they are best suited for incorporation into concrete pond designs. Despite their undoubted inconvenience, large constructed internal pond filters are very good at their job. If they were not, they would not be as popular as they are with Koi keepers who demand the highest standards of water quality.

Recent years have seen the introduction of a range of manufactured internal pond filters which combine the proven advantage of the constructed type with few, if any, of its disadvantages.

Some of the newer internal models consist of compact units supplied with inflow and outflow pipes which allow them to be introduced into an existing pump circuit, usually at some point (below water) between the pump outlet and a fountain or watercourse outflow. The beauty of these in-line internal filters is that they can be removed quickly and serviced with the minimum of disruption. Ponds of 4500 liters (1000 Imp. gals) capacity, or even more, can be efficiently filtered by the larger filters of this type.

Many manufactured internal filters are designed on a combination of two basic principles which are well-known to aquarists, i.e. those used in foam and undergravel filtration systems.

These internal pond filters can be operated by both surface and submersible pumps. Since they are fitted to the pump inflow, they work by sucking dirty water through one or more filter media (usually two.) Removable open-foam cartridges are generally fitted on to a series of perforated intake tubes which sit above a sealed bottom unit (looking something like a plastic cistern) containing gravel, foam (which may be zeolite-impregnated), or some other suitable medium. An outflow pipe protruding from the base of the bottom unit then takes the now clean water to the pump and thence to the fountain or watercourse in the normal way.

Though these internal filters are more cumbersome than the in-line models mentioned above, they can be more effective. They are also more easily serviced than constructed/permanent internal filters. This has, no doubt, been one of the major factors responsible for their increase in popularity in the last few years.

Despite the somewhat different ways in which the various systems outlined above filter dirty water, they all share, at least, one common feature, i.e. they drive water through a filtering medium. This obviously reduces the amount of water available to feed a fountain or watercourse, an important fact to bear in mind when choosing a pond pump.

External Filters There never seems to be just one single way of doing things in pondkeeping. Choices exist virtually everywhere, and filtration is no exception. Pondkeepers who, for whatever reason, feel that internal filters do not provide them with the ideal solution to water purification may find external systems considerably more acceptable.

Disabled or elderly pondowners, in particular, should find the ease of access to external filters very much in their favor.

One disadvantage that all external systems possess is that they need to be hidden from view, or else developed into a positive feature,

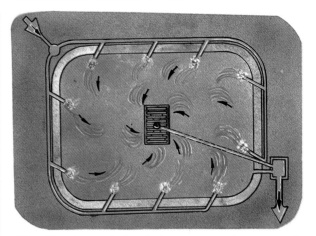

The filtration and circulation system of your pond, as with the pond itself, can be as vast, complex, or simple as meets your needs—and the needs of your pond.

e.g. by placing them inside a model mill house or behind a large rocky outcrop.

External filtration systems can be constructed or bought. Constructed models often turn out to be cheaper and can be built to individual specifications. Whichever option you choose, the principle remains the same since dirty water has to be passed through a filtering medium, just as in an internal filter. In fact, some manufactured pond filters are so similar in function that they can be used internally or externally. If you decide to put your own external system together, you have a choice.

Concrete You could, for example, construct your own concrete filter. In one type, water is forced through the medium from below (as in an aquarium reverse-flow undergravel filter), while in the other, the pump simply pours the dirty water onto the surface of the filtering chamber and leaves the rest to gravity (as in aquarium trickle filters.)

Of the two systems, the former can generally turn over a larger volume of water than the latter. This does not necessarily increase its level of biological activity though, but it does increase the rate at which water can be mechanically filtered.

In the gravity-acting system, the rate at which water is pumped into the filter chamber needs to be adjusted so that it equals the maximum rate at which it can flow out under the force of gravity. This makes the gravity model just a little more finicky to install.

The pump that services your fountain or other water feature can, if powerful enough, also service your pond filter.

Plastic External filters can also be constructed of plastic components (with the odd non-corrosive, non-toxic tap/valve thrown in.) At its simplest, all that is required is a plastic container, such as a household cistern with a lid, plastic inlet and outlet pipes, one or two valves and one or more types of filter media.

One of the pipes is usually fitted near the top edge of the cistern and the other near the base on the opposite side. The cistern is then filled with filter medium and one of the pipes (the inlet) is connected to the pond pump outlet. The other filter pipe forms the outlet (see below.) The flow-rate through the filter is determined by the capacity of the pump itself and by the valves installed in the inlet and/or outlet pipes.

If the filter pipe connected to the pond pump outlet is the top one, this will act as the filter inlet and will result in normal biological filtration/purification. If the bottom one is linked to the pump outlet instead, this one will act as the filter inlet and will result in reverse-flow filtration.

The basic model can be modified and refined considerably according to needs and preferences. This has naturally been followed up by manufacturers who have produced a wide variety of models, ranging from the very basic to the very sophisticated.

ADVICE IS IMPORTANT

Many petshops have working displays of filters, pumps and fountains, so it is well worth paying them a visit before you invest in or construct your own filter. Besides allowing you to get an idea of what your envisaged system will look like, a visit to a specialist pet dealer also gives you an opportunity to get expert advice.

Key matters you would need to discuss in connection with your filtration system should include:

1. The best size/type of filter for your pond. This will be influenced by the size of the pond, its inhabitants, general layout, presence/absence of watercourses, fountains, etc.
2. The most suitable location for your filter in terms of height above/below the water surface, distance away from the pond, and so on.
3. The most appropriate pump for your set-up, bearing in mind the points mentioned in (2), plus other relevant factors such as restriction in the flow-rate caused by the type and amount of filter medium.

If you are going to install a filter, you might as well install the best possible system you can afford. There seems little point then in basing your decisions on guesswork. Seek advice from the specialists to suit your circumstances.

DRAINS

Most ponds do not require the installation of drains. In fact, some types of pond cannot easily be fitted with drains, though this does not necessarily mean they cannot, or should not, be installed. It simply means that the decision to incorporate one in a water scheme cannot be taken lightly.

Lined ponds, for example, can be fitted with drains but special attachments must be used to ensure that the hole which has to be cut to accommodate the drain-plug is watertight. Then, since a drain hole has to be located at the deepest point, the decision whether or not to opt for one must be made during the earliest stages of pond planning.

Some of the first questions one should ask about this subject are:

- What job does a drain actually do?
- Can this job be done just as effectively in some other, easier way?
- If so, does my pond really need a drain?
- If it doesn't, how badly do I want to include a drain in my pond design?

From the above, you will see that a major factor could be whether or not you actually want to incorporate draining facilities into your design.

As far as the job aspect is concerned, a drain provides a very effective means of removing mulm and debris from the bottom of a pond, provided the bottom slopes towards the plug-hole.

If crystal-clear water is required at all times, as in Koi ponds, the installation of a drain is an undoubted advantage. These beautiful fish look their best when they are large, but an unavoidable consequence of being large (and being a carp, as Koi are) is that the intake of food, and the inevitable output of wastes, are correspondingly large. Drains can, obviously, provide a most efficient means of removing these solid wastes. However, waste disposal can also be carried out quite effectively by other methods. Nowadays, there are hand or electrically operated pond 'vacuum cleaners' which can suck up mulm and debris, in the same way they have been used to clean swimming pools.

Major clean-outs can also be carried out by pumping the water out of the pond with an ordinary pond pump. While this will remove most of the water, it will still leave a large part of the accumulated mulm behind. Removing this sludge is not the most pleasant of jobs and, coupled with the fishes' and plants' need for alternative accommodation, argues strongly for the regular removal of debris as it builds up.

If you opt for built-in drainage, bear in mind that structural weaknesses can develop unless the system is planned thoroughly. Some of the deeper types of prefabricated ponds have special reinforced panels specifically designed to accommodate a drain, so it is well worth having a look at these before making your final decision.

Whatever system is used, it must be watertight. If water seeps out, it will eventually erode some of the underlying soil or supporting material. This, in turn, could well undermine the whole pond with disastrous consequences.

In this koi pond, located outside a Japanese hotel, the filter is huge in relation to the size of the pond. This is because koi require high-quality water. The capacity of your pond filter will be determined in part by your choice of pond inhabitants.

KOSHIHARA METHOD

Alternatively, you could use the Koshihara method, which does not undermine a pond through subsoil erosion. It works very well in ponds where the water is not heavily laden with solid wastes, uses the pressure of the water in the pond itself and does not even require the installation of a pump. It is well suited to ponds with a sloping bottom, with or without a drainage sump. The outflow can be controlled quite easily by means of a plug or a valve in the outlet pipe. Either way, the main principle is that the outflow is located outside the pond but below water level. As soon as the plug is removed or the valve is opened, pressure will force debris-laden water from the bottom of the pond or drainage sump up through the outlet pipe and away to waste.

This is an ingenious but effective method which, like all other drainage systems, needs to be incorporated into the overall plan for a pond from the very outset. The only problem is that if it leaks or is opened by a child, it might drain the entire pond with disastrous results!

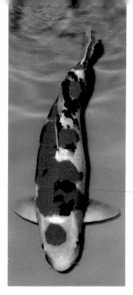

次 席 12部 大正三色
受賞者 畑中　泰(兵庫県)

次 席 12部 大正三色
受賞者 手塚孝司(神奈川県)

次 席 12部 昭和三色
受賞者 大浜忠次(神奈川県)

次 席 12部 写りもの
受賞者 阪井養魚場(広島県)

次 席 12部 写りもの
受賞者 河野久仁雄(群馬県)

次 席 13部 紅　白
受賞者 手塚孝司(神奈川県)

次 席 13部 紅　白
受賞者 加藤柾男(栃木県)

次 席 13部 紅　白
受賞者 昭　徳苑(広島県)

次 席 13部 大正三色
受賞者 佐藤秀一(三重県)

次 席 13部 大正三色
受賞者 二川昭二(京都府)

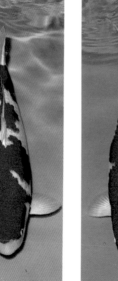

次 席 13部 写りもの

次 席 13部 写りもの

次 席 14部 紅　白

次 席 14部 紅　白

次 席 14部 紅　白

10

Stocking a Pond

If you visit a water garden center, particularly when the coldwater fish season is in full swing, you cannot help being bowled over by the range and colors of fish, plants and pond products available. Even well-established pondkeepers are, fortunately, not immune from this feeling of excitement. I, for one, take great delight in wandering round these centers and don't mind admitting that I invariably lapse into a stage of wishful thinking....if only my pond were larger, or if it were of this type, or that, I could then introduce such-and-such a fish or establish such-and-such a display of plants, or incorporate this type of waterfall, or cascade.

Fortunately, common-sense always prevails. Experience has taught me, and millions like me, that rash decisions, based purely on emotions, often have distressing consequences. It definitely pays to know what your needs are before you buy fish and plants.

SAFE ENVIRONMENTS

Ensure that your pond is *safe* before you introduce any livestock, and that you are fully aware of the needs and habits of your proposed pond inhabitants.

In an earlier section dealing with concrete and block ponds, I considered the toxic qualities of cement and outlined several techniques for making such ponds safe for aquatic plants and fish.

Lined and prefabricated ponds are, of course, free of these dangers, but it would be a mistake to think that they are completely safe for stocking as soon as they are filled with water. While liners, fiberglass and other well-known non-cement products do not contaminate water in any way, the raw water used to fill a pond can, itself, represent a hostile environment for many forms of aquatic life.

Facing Page: Koi are immensely popular in Japan. As is seen in this page taken from a specialty magazine in Japan, the color varieties of koi are numerous—only a small protion of the many different varieties available are shown here.

ADDITIVES

One of the main sources of danger lies in the treatment tapwater receives to make it safe for human consumption. Chlorine is the best-known of the 'protective' additives, but chloramine can also be added to supplies, particularly during periods of water shortage.

Chemicals such as sodium thiosulphate can be mixed with tapwater to neutralize these additives quickly (though chloramine-treated water also needs to be passed through an ammonia-absorbing medium), but this should prove unnecessary if the prospective pond-owner can be a bit patient.

Recently, a new compound capable of neutralizing chloramine and chlorine safely and quickly in both marine and freshwater environments has been developed in the USA.

Chlorine, for instance, is quite volatile and will usually dissipate within a day or so. Water movement by means of fountains and waterfalls can encourage this process, but several days of circulation and exposure to the air should be considered an absolute minimum before fish are added.

Chloramine is considerably less volatile and will take over a week to dissipate naturally. What is more, one of the intermediate compounds formed when chloramine is broken down is ammonia, already referred to under Biological Purification as a highly effective fish killer.

Ammonia can be removed quickly and inexpensively from aquaria using absorbing materials like zeolite, but the amount of zeolite usually needed for a pond can make the exercise rather costly. However, zeolite-impregnated foam can reduce costs considerably. Even so, since time (which is free) will dissipate ammonia in a

To maintain a safe environment for your fish, the use of a test kit is advised.

number of ways (including biological breakdown), it makes sense to be patient.

Efficient micro-biological activity takes many weeks to develop, so you cannot really depend on this method in a brand-new pond. In fact,

Hornwort, Ceratophyllum demersum, *is a submerged plant that can be included in your pond.*

even if you have a well established biological filter in your pond, it will not be able to cope quickly with the relatively large flood of ammonia released when a major overhaul is carried out using water treated with chloramine. At such times zeolite-containing foam really comes into its own.

OXYGENATING PLANTS

Submerged oxygenating plants absorb many chemicals from the water, including metallic salts. Raw tapwater just happens to be relatively rich in these substances. Therefore, it follows that adding several substantial bunches of oxygenating plants like Hornwort (*Ceratophyllum demersum*), Elodea (*Elodea canadensis*) or Crispa (*Lagarosiphon major*) will prove extremely helpful in taking the hard edge from tapwater.

FISH STOCKING LEVELS

Assuming you have followed the above guidelines, you will soon end up with a crystal-clear, very young, but safe, pond which is ready for stocking. You should have a pretty good idea by now what sorts of fish you are going to have. Details of the most suitable (and some not so suitable) species and varieties are given later.

The crucial thing at the stocking stage is working out how many fish your pond can comfortably accommodate. It is important to accept from the word 'GO' that we can't fool nature. It, and not we, will eventually determine the size of our pond population. We can help things along by adequate aeration and filtration, but we can never force nature beyond its limits. So it is pointless fighting against its laws. We might as well obey the rules. We owe it to our fish.

To be on the safe side, we can apply the following basic stocking rule:

Allow 24 sq. in. (155 cm^2) of pond surface for every 1 in. (2.5 cm) of fish, excluding the tail (at 70°F = 21°C.)

Using this rule-of-thumb, and employing the traditional Imperial calculations normally used for estimating stocking levels (and therefore given first in this example), a pond measuring 10 ft x 5 ft (3 m x 1.5 m) would have a surface area of 5O sq. ft. (4.5 sq.m.) This works out at 7200 sq. in and 45000 sq. cm respectively. Given the 24 sq.

The stocking potential of a given pond is directly related to the volume of water, the surface area, the temperature, and the filtration and oxygenation systems of the pond. These factors must be considered before you stock your pond.

in. stocking rule, it follows that a pond of this size can take:

$$\underline{7200} \text{ in } (\underline{4500} \times 2.5 \text{ cm}) \text{ of fish, i.e., 300 in. or}$$
$$24 \qquad 155 \qquad \text{around 725 cm.}$$

When 45000 is divided by 155, the resulting figure represents the number of 155 'units' available for stocking. Since each of these can accommodate about 2.5 cm of fish, the figure obtained from dividing 45000 by 155, i.e. 290, needs to be multiplied by 2.5 to produce the final stocking figure of around 725 cm of fish. It must be remembered, though, that these results always allow for some flexibility. The warmer the water, the fewer the fish!

How you split up this allowance is up to you. You could have 30 x 10 in (approx. 25 cm) specimens, or 300 x 1 in specimens (approx. 2.5 cm), or any other permutation in between, but only if the maximum temperature of the water is 70°F. or lower; at 80°F, the capacity is half.

One very important factor to bear in mind, though, is that, if you go too close to your stocking limit at the outset, you will almost certainly end up well over it later. So, in theory, one should base one's calculations on the eventual maximum size of the chosen fish. In practice, this can easily result in quite an empty-looking pond. To be truthful, 20 colorful 6 in (15 cm) Goldfish or Koi look quite impressive but 120 1 in (2.5 cm) olive-brown specimens (most Goldfish and Koi are this color when small) can look very ordinary.

Many people compromise in various ways. One option is to buy a mixture of large and small specimens. Another alternative is to stock close to the limit with largish fish and pass some on to other pondkeeping friends, or sell them to a local retailer, in due course.

GUIDE TO STOCKING LEVELS

So far, I have only referred to surface area as a deciding factor in calculating stocking levels. Volume also plays a part, but is less important. The reason is quite logical.

Oxygen dissolves into the water at the surface, so the larger the surface area, the higher its oxygen-absorbing properties. Clearly, then, the larger the surface area, the larger the number of fish a pond can safely house. Fountains, waterfalls and other similar features agitate the water surface and help it absorb oxygen. In addition, submerged plants release oxygen during the hours of daylight through a process known as photosynthesis. Taking all the above into consideration, we can draw several broad conclusions:

1. If two ponds hold equal volumes of water but have different surface areas, the one with the larger surface area will be able to accommodate more fish. The colder the water, the more fish can be accommodated, too.
2. If two ponds have identical surface area and volume dimensions, but one has a fountain, waterfall, watercourse, cascade, filter or any other water aerating/purifying feature, such as a Venturi system, then the pond with the additional feature(s) will be able to hold more fish.

(A Venturi attachment consists of a length of airline extending from a pump intake up to the water surface. This allows the pump to suck in atmospheric air and later expel it as bubbles in the outflow.)

3. If two ponds are identical in dimensions and aerating/purifying features, but only one contains an adequate complement of submerged plants, the pond with the vegetation will be able to house more fish.
4. If two ponds are identical in every way except water depth, then the deeper pond will, within limits, accommodate more fish.

PLANT STOCKING LEVELS

During the hours of daylight, submerged aquatic plants generate oxygen as a by-product of photosynthesis, a process virtually unique to green plants, though there are also some photosynthetic bacteria. In photosynthesis, carbon dioxide is absorbed by the leaves and combined, through the action of sunlight, with molecules of water to produce carbohydrates. All organisms require carbohydrates, but only photosynthetic ones can generate them. The others, fish and humans alike, obtain their supplies directly or indirectly from plants.

Therefore, in a pond in the presence of sunlight only, submerged aquatic plants help maintain good water conditions by absorbing potentially harmful carbon dioxide and generating life-giving

Green plants help to remove wastes from the pond environment. They also release oxygen during the process of photosynthesis. Do not, however, rely on plants to do the jobs that only mechanical devices can perform.

oxygen in the process. While they are photosynthesizing, plants continue to respire and, in so doing, use up some of the oxygen they generate. But in a well-planted pond, oxygen production generally outstrips the rate at which it is absorbed by the plants. The net result is that actively photosynthesizing plants oxygenate the water, helping to maintain favorable environmental conditions, both for themselves and the other pond inhabitants.

Plants also absorb a wide range of dissolved chemicals from the water, some of which can be dangerous to animal life above certain concentrations. A valuable spin-off from this is that some of the chemicals absorbed are precisely those required by algae. Submerged plants are therefore a very effective natural method of controlling algae. Submerged vegetation also provides shelter for fish, including fry, and acts as a spawning medium for many species. All in all, oxygenating plants are highly desirable, stabilizing (buffering) members of most pond communities.

The main exception to this rule is found in those Koi ponds where top priority is given to keeping the fish in full view all the time. Dense clumps of submerged vegetation will then be seen as unnecessary obstacles. Since excellent aeration and filtration systems are usually installed in the best-kept Koi ponds anyway, the need for natural oxygenators and purifiers is not as great as in more conventional ponds. Koi usually eat the plants anyway, and a luxuriant growth of submerged plants does not usually coexist very long with large Koi.

Pond profiles don't tend to conform to rigid rules, and actual bottom areas available for planting are likely to vary from pond to pond, so relating plant stocking areas to surface volume can't be done the way it is with fish. As a rough guide, the stocking level should be 20 plants for a pond with a surface area of up to 100 square feet, 10 plants for a pond between 100 and 500 square feet, and 6 plants for a pond of above 500 square feet. Note that recommended pond stocking levels decrease as the size of the pond increases. This is quite logical because larger ponds are generally more stable than smaller ones, have a greater surface area (for oxygen absorption and carbon dioxide elimination), contain more water, and so on. In other words, larger ponds are likely to be less prone to potentially harmful fluctuations than small ones.

There are three other groups of plants associated with ponds:

Floating Plants These have floating leaves and roots suspended in midwater. Examples are Duckweed (*Lemna* spp), Fairy Moss (*Azolla caroliniana*) and Water Soldier (*Stratiotes aloides*.)

Surface Plants These have floating leaves and anchored roots. The best examples are Water Lilies (*Nymphaea* spp), but there are many others, such as the Water Hawthorn (*Aponogeton distachyus*) and the Water Fringe (*Nymphoides peltata*.)

Marginal Plants Marginal plants are usually referred to as marginals; they have roots anchored underwater (or in moist ground) and aerial leaves. There are many species and varieties, e.g., Marsh Marigold *(Caltha palustris),* Dwarf Reed Mace or Dwarf Bulrush *(Typha minima)* and Cotton Grass *(Eriophorum* spp.)

Of these three groups, the last has little, if any, influence on water conditions in terms of surface cover. The main role played by marginals in a water scheme is esthetic, although they contribute in other ways by absorbing chemicals through their roots and providing pupating sites for the last nymphal stages of some aquatic insects (as well as perches for the adults.)

Plants can be potted to eliminate the need for a planting medium to be laid across the entire bottom of the pond.

Floating and surface Plants, on the other hand, have a profound influence on water conditions. They can, for instance, make the difference between green algal-laden water and crystal-clear conditions, simply by controlling the amount of light that reaches the pond surface. On average, 60% surface cover in the form of floating and/or surface plants, coupled with adequate stocks of submerged aquatic vegetation and a good maintenance regime should reduce green water problems to a minimum.

By shading the water from the sun, floating leaves help to keep ponds cooler than they would otherwise be. This is particularly important in warm countries and during prolonged hot periods in temperate areas. Goldfish and many other pond fish can withstand relatively high temperatures for some time but, if this becomes excessive, they soon begin to show signs of distress, reduced resistance to some diseases and even loss of appetite.

While it is generally appreciated that surface vegetation prevents heat and light getting into the pond, it is hardly ever noted that it also prevents water getting out of the pond in the form of evaporation. The amount may be insignificant in cool, damp weather, but certainly not so—especially in small ponds—when it is hot and dry. This becomes all the more significant when such periods are likely to coincide with school summer vacation when most people take their holidays. While they are away sunning themselves, their fish could be 'boiling' back at home! When water evaporates from the pond, it cools it at the same time.

Bricks or blocks can serve as shelves to raise marginals to a point closer to the surface of the water.

PLANTING TECHNIQUES
SUBMERGED OXYGENATING PLANTS

With the exception of Hornwort *(Ceratophyllum),* submerged oxygenating plants form roots with which they anchor themselves to the substratum. However, they can only anchor themselves if there is a substratum. Sufficient mulm and debris will accumulate in due course to provide such a rooting medium, but this will take some time, so it is advisable to bed the plants in from the start in sand or aquarium gravel placed in seed trays or other suitable containers.

This will give them the headstart they need. If time allows for planting to be carried out several weeks before fish are introduced, root growth should be sufficiently well established to prevent the plants being pulled out by scavenging fish.

SURFACE PLANTS

Surface plants such as Water Lilies should be planted in special plant baskets or perforated pots. If they are planted in baskets, then these should be lined with hessian, burlap, or some other suitable material (see below.) Several points are worth noting:

- Hessian (sacking) will rot in due course and will need to be replaced. Plastic mesh or liberally perforated polyethylene will last longer.
- A base layer of stones will help stabilize the planting basket—particularly important with marginal plants.

Duckweed, Lemna *sp., is a floating plant found in many ponds. It is considered a pest by some, but a welcome inhabitant by others.*

Ponds and pools located in warm, moist climates have the tendency of inviting a lush growth of plantlife. Garden ponds located in these climates will probably require a 'weeding' of excessive plant growth.

- Suitable planting media are closely cropped turf, garden soil or loam. Avoid peat and fertilizer-rich soils. Special fertilizer blocks are available, however.
- A layer of gravel laid on top of the compacted planting medium will protect the soil from grubbing fish and help keep down water turbidity.
- The crowns of surface plants must project slightly above soil level. (They could rot if covered up.)
- Old roots and leaves should be removed when planting.
- The eventual size of a Water Lily must be checked and matched with an appropriately sized basket. Small types, such as the Pygmy Water Lilies, e.g. *Nymphaea pygmaea helvola,* can be comfortably planted in a 6 in x 6 in (15 cm x 15 cm) basket. At the other extreme, *Nymphaea alba* needs a square container measuring about 15-18 in (38-45 cm.)

When planting has been completed, lower the basket gently into position. If a basket is plunged into the pond, much of the painstaking work done beforehand will be spoilt.

Two people may be needed to lower baskets into the deeper parts of the pond (which are also usually furthest from the edge.) If no help is available, this can be done by laying a plank across the pond and lowering the basket into position from there. I would only advise using this technique if you know you can keep your balance!

One final point. It is always wise to check on the preferred water depth of the various species or varieties of surface plants you have chosen for your pond before you lower the baskets into position. While it is usually possible to get away with shallower conditions than the ideal recommended for most surface plants, the reverse does not generally apply. Excessively deep water usually results in poor growth.

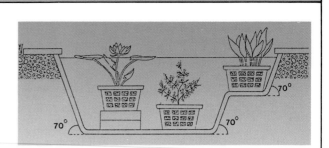

Left and Above: Marginals can be planted in baskets (above), or allowed to grow as they will (left). Either way they are a handsome addition to the pond setting.

MARGINAL PLANTS

The basic planting technique for marginals is the same as for surface plants. One major difference between them is that the leaves of marginal plants stand upright into the air, while those of surface plants, as their name suggests, lie flat on top of the water. So, even in protected places, marginal plants will be at the mercy of the elements and can topple over quite easily if subjected to strong winds, particularly if they are tall and/or overcrowded in an undersized pot. Several steps can be taken to minimize this risk:

1. The layer of stones placed on the bottom of the container can be made deeper for marginals than for surface plants.
2. Alternatively, or in addition, heavier stones can be chosen.
3. Straight-sided planting containers can be used rather than those with the more conventional tapered sides.
4. The container can be supported all around the outside with bricks or flat-bottomed rocks.
5. Baskets or pots holding the tallest plants can be placed in the most sheltered spots.
6. A regular check can be kept on the growth of the plants, so they can be thinned out as necessary to avoid overcrowding.
7. The restraint of the water can be used to help hold up the plants by placing the containers as close to the deepest recommended levels for individual plants as possible.

On this last point, it is worth noting that marginals respond in the same way to water depth as surface plants, i.e. you can get away with over-shallow planting, but not usually with excessively deep conditions.

Below: Plant baskets can be lowered as shown.

One of the advantages of planting baskets is that they can be easily removed from the pond and thus allow the more delicate species of pond plants (such as some water lilies) to be over wintered in a more suitable environment. They can then be easily replanted in the following spring.

PLANTING TECHNIQUES AND WILDLIFE PONDS

The use of planting containers may make life easier for the pond owner and has much to recommend it. But in wildlife ponds, the use of pots and baskets seems to go against the spirit of such a water scheme.

Plants don't grow in nice little clumps in the wild either. They spread, and it is extremely difficult to create this illusion if the plants are artificially restricted. Anyway, if the guidelines given earlier in the book for installing and filling wildlife ponds have been followed, the sides and bottom should be covered in soil or rooting medium, thereby providing an ideal anchoring and growing substratum for submerged, surface and marginal plants.

One welcome and natural consequence of this approach is that the 'toppling over' problem is eliminated completely.

The use of planting containers may make life easier for the pond owner and has much to recommend it. But in wildlife ponds, the use of pots and baskets seems to go against the spirit of such a water scheme.

11

Buying, Quarantining and Introducing Fish

BUYING FISH

There are a few signs that one can look for when buying fish. If, for example, several fish in a holding trough or tank look decidedly unhealthy, it is best to forget buying any fish, however healthy they look, from the same batch. It is not worth taking the risk.

Some good pointers to watch out for in healthy fish are:

- Erect fins (except in some long-finned varieties)
- Lively disposition
- Balanced swimming
- Full body
- Good appetite
- Intact fins, i.e. no tears
- No missing scales
- No injuries, lumps or sores

If you buy a fish with these characteristics, the chances are you have bought a healthy fish. Some internal diseases are not detectable in the early phases, so you can never be 100 per cent certain of a fish's state of health, but the above should give you a good start.

QUARANTINE

Nowadays, many aquatic pet shops sell fully quarantined stocks for ponds and aquaria. It is therefore well worthwhile checking on this whenever you buy fish for initial or subsequent stocking.

If the first batch of fish has already been quarantined, it should be quite safe to introduce them into the pond without a further period of isolation. In fact, the pond itself can be used as quarantine quarters for the very first lot of fish. Obviously, it is always wise to keep a close watch on things for the first week or so to make sure that everything is in order.

If any fish requires treatment, this should be carried out in a separate pond, trough or aquarium, while the main pond is treated with a general preventive remedy. All fish bought subsequently should undergo a period of quarantine lasting at least a week, but preferably two or more, during which they can be observed and treated if necessary. These fish must not be introduced into the main pond until you have made certain that they are not carrying any pathogenic (disease-causing) organisms. Treatment with proprietary anti-fluke and anti-bacterial remedies (following directions to the letter) should reduce risks to an absolute minimum

INTRODUCING FISH

Introducing fish into a pond involves more than just tearing open the plastic bag in which they have been transported and pouring them in. In fact, if you do this, you are soon likely to regret it.

There are many diseases that can attack a fish, and many of them are inconspicuous to the unobservant eye. The koi in the photo below has an infection noticeable because of the white blotches on the head of the fish.

Goldfish are a very popular fish found in garden pools. Goldfish, like koi, come in many color varieties. Remember that if your pond is to house fish and will be subjected to extremes in temperature, it will need to be sufficiently deep to prevent complete freezing or rapid temperature swings.

In the first place, fish should not be carried home in an unwrapped plastic bag. This will only add to the level of stress already induced through netting. A little protection, such as a paper bag, newspaper or insulated polystyrene box will help enormously in settling a fish down. Having got home, carry out the following steps:

1. Float the bag in the pond for about 15 minutes (up to one hour if the volume of water is large) to allow the temperature of the 'bag' water to rise or fall gradually to that of the pond. Never float a bag in a pond without protecting it in some way from overheating if the day is hot and sunny

2. Untie the bag—do not burst it—and mix in a small amount of pond water, ending up with a mixture of about 1 part pond water to 3 parts bag water.

3. Leave the bag in the pond for a further 10 minutes, resting the open end on the pond surround and weighing it down with a rock.

4. Repeat (2) and (3) at least once more. This allows the fish to get used to their new water chemistry in several small stages.

5. Gently tip out the fish into the pond. Avoid pouring them in.

POND MAINTENANCE

A new pond takes time to mature. Some say that it takes at least one whole season, or even a year. Irrespective of how long it takes to become fully mature, changes begin to occur from the moment water is introduced into an empty pond.

The art of pond maintenance lies in keeping all conditions within tolerable limits. Ensuring that stocking levels are not exceeded and that proper quarantine and introduction procedures are followed, will, obviously, go a long way towards this.

Equally important is the establishment of a sound maintenance regime. The most effective way of doing this is by getting to know the needs of your fish and plants, the potential of your chosen system, and the techniques available to prevent things going wrong, or remedying them effectively if they do.

FISH AND PLANTS

As far as the needs of the fish and plants are concerned, food, oxygen and reasonable environmental conditions are the three main factors contributing to success or failure. Fish foods and feeding require further discussion.

FEEDING FISH

As a visit to any fish shop will prove, there is really no excuse for *any* fish to go hungry. There is such a wide range of dry flakes, fry foods, mini-pellets, jumbo pellets, frozen and freeze-dried foods, livefoods and other feeds available that, if there is a problem at all, it is in deciding which food best meets the needs of your fish. A word or two with a member of the shop or staff will soon put you right.

Most pond fish are omnivorous, i.e. they will eat both plant and animal matter. A few, such as Orfe *(Leuciscus idus),* are predominantly carnivorous (flesh eaters.) Yet even these will take Goldfish or Koi pellets regularly; so there really is no problem in providing an adequate diet. Just choose sensibly and all should be well.

As for the quantity per feed, at all costs avoid overfeeding. Foods that claim not to cloud water are simply misleading. *All* uneaten food eventually rots and clouds the water. Uneaten food will lead to a deterioration of water conditions. A good way of avoiding overfeeding is to follow what I call 'the five-minute rule'. According to this, *the correct amount of food is that which will be completely consumed within five minutes.*

During the growing season, five or even six such feeds per day may be necessary. But this demand will vanish between late autumn (fall) and early spring when no food at all should be given. Once the temperature of the water drops below 4.5°C (40°F), pond fish are virtually unable to digest food. So there is no point in trying to feed them at such times. In fact, serious health problems can develop if partly digested food remains in a fish's gut for a lengthy period.

Just as fish change during the course of a year, so do plants. They grow, spread, flower, die, get eaten, and so on. If ignored, they will not only suffer, but they could also affect the condition of the water and, ultimately, the fish. A good maintenance routine will go a long way towards minimizing risks.

There are two factors that must be balanced when feeding your fish: (1) avoid over-feeding, as over feeding will result in excessive polluting of the pond; and (2) be sure that all of your fish receive a sufficient quantity of food. It is easy to over-feed, and it is easy for bullies to consume all food before the more timid fish get a chance to eat.

Pelleted foods like the one shown above, especially floating pelleted foods, offer a clean and efficient way of providing for the dietary requirements of pond fish.

THE CHANGING SEASONS

The following is a guide to the main areas of activity which require attention during the course of a full calendar year. It should provide a means of avoiding disasters, but should be adapted as necessary to meet your own circumstances.

SPRING

This is traditionally regarded as the start of the pondkeeping season. In practice, early spring is a time of little visible activity. Fish are rather sluggish and plant growth limited at best (except for the Marsh Marigold, *Caltha palustris.)* Feed fish very sparingly at first, and only when they show signs of active searching.

A partial water change should be carried out, either by siphoning out some water and replacing it gradually with tapwater, or by running a trickle of water into the pond and allowing it to overflow for a number of hours. Either way, the use of a proprietary dechlorinator and water conditioner is advisable. Mid-spring is characterized by a higher level of activity among the fish and plants. Fish can now be fed regularly (but in small amounts at first.)

Pondwater may turn green but do resist the temptation to carry out a further water change. This will only introduce a new supply of mineral salts which the algae will feed on to reproduce to epidemic levels in a very short time. It is preferable to wait and allow natural growth of submerged and surface plants to absorb nutrients from the water and shade it sufficiently to discourage algal growth. Algicide tablets, slow-release blocks and liquid treatments are all available and can be used to produce quick, if somewhat temporary, results.

Filamentous algae which form dense clumps and are collectively referred to as Blanket Weed, can present problems during spring (or in stagnant water at other times.) Removal by hand, or by rotating a cleft stick in each clump, is an essential first step. The avoidance of still, standing water (particularly in shallow areas), plus adequate growth of normal plants, will subsequently keep Blanket Weed under control.

Spawning will begin in spring and stretch into summer. Bunches of fine-leaved vegetation or spawning mats containing Koi eggs can either be removed to a second pond or an aquarium where hatching can take place in relative safety, or be left in the pond where eggs and fry will have to take their chances, just as they do in the wild.

Late spring is a good time for planting, or for a general clean-out of an established pond. It must be remembered, though, that a re-filled, overhauled pond is, in effect, a new pond and will require time to mature and settle down. By late spring, the fish will be feeding well and should receive several feeds per day.

SUMMER

Planting can continue throughout summer when plant growth is at its most vigorous. Some pests such as leeches, dragonfly nymphs, water boatmen and diving beetles are just as vigorous. No pool can be regarded as immune from these creatures. Fortunately, they generally do little damage. Most of the leeches found in ponds

Spring is when the garden pond hobby begins to reach full stride.

Diving beetles and their larvae can pose quite a threat, even to sizable fish. With the use of a net, however, they can be scooped out of the water when they surface to breathe.

tend to feed on organisms such as snails, rather than on fish. They can usually be kept under control by baiting with meat or liver enclosed in such a way that fish cannot get at this potential food source.

Particularly bad infestations can be eliminated by draining the pond and keeping it absolutely dry for at least several weeks—hardly the sort of situation one would relish. Nowadays there are also some trichlorphon-based 'anti-leech' proprietary treatments available. These preparations must, however, be used with caution since some species of fish, such as Orfe, are quite sensitive to chemicals and can react badly to even a small overdose.

Diving beetles and their larvae can pose quite a threat, even to sizeable fish. Unfortunately, there is no quick, easy way of eliminating them. However, both adults and larvae need to surface for air and can be lifted out with a swift flick of a hand net (easier said than done!) Water boatmen pose less of a threat but can be treated in the same way. If it is possible to cover the

entire surface of the pond with fine-meshed screening to prevent the beetles from getting air, they will die.

Dragonfly and Damselfly nymphs feed on all sorts of small animals, including fry, but not on adult fish, so they do not present an intolerable problem. Without wishing to offend purists, I must say that I welcome the sight of Dragonflies and Damselflies flying around my own ponds. When it comes to wildlife ponds, no such system could be regarded complete without these airborne visitors. Dragonflies eat mosquitoes!

Among the fish, spawning will continue throughout the summer, and feeding can be carried out almost on demand. I feed my own fish five or six times a day—keeping to the five-minute rule. But once a day is sufficient, too.

Plant pests, such as some midges, caterpillars and beetles, rarely cause serious damage to ponds which are well stocked with fish. If treatment is required, removal or submergence (for several days) of the affected leaves usually proves adequate. Badly infected plants should be removed from the pond and given a gentle dose of insecticide elsewhere.

Regular cleaning of the pond bottom will also help during summer.

AUTUMN (FALL)

Fish will feed quite avidly well into autumn, so it is important to keep up the supply of food until they show signs of slowing down. Properly fed fish stand a much better chance of surviving the winter than underfed ones (if the temperature drops significantly in late autumn, feeding should cease altogether.)

The pond may need protecting against leaf fall from surrounding trees and shrubs during mid to late autumn. Alternatively, remove the leaves several times each day. Submerged oxygenators can be cut back at any time, since growth will have virtually stopped by mid-autumn. Dead leaves and blooms should also be removed from surface plants, while marginals can be tidied up.

A partial water change, like that suggested for spring, will be found very beneficial.

WINTER

Once winter arrives, feeding should cease completely until the next spring. If the fish have

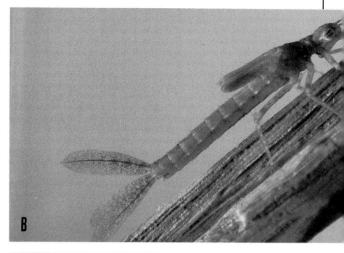

A. *Dragonfly nymph,* Aeschna *sp.*
B. *Damselfly larva,* Lestes *sp.*
C. *Caddisfly larva,* Limnephilus *sp.*
D. *Mayfly larva,* Baetis *sp.*

been fed properly so far, they will have built up adequate reserves to take them through in a state of virtual suspended animation. Ice will form on the water surface with increasing regularity through winter. If the covering is thin, it will, at least, partially thaw out each day and be no problem, but persistent ice can prevent the escape of toxic gases from the pond.

Winter deaths are more likely to be the result of poisoning or lack of oxygen than cold, so some way of keeping part of the water surface ice-free is needed. The most permanent way of achieving this is by using a pond heater to keep a sufficiently large hole open for effective gas dispersal at all times, however cold the weather might get.

One or more squeezable balls floating on the surface will also help keep small areas ice-free. All you need to do is remove the balls in the morning and replace them later on in the day before new ice forms. Very light balls, e.g. beach balls, are not much use, and even heavier balls will only prove partially effective in severe weather, when compared to a good pond heater.

In principle, a similar effect can be obtained by floating a polystyrene box or plastic bottle (ballasted with a few stones) on the surface. The box can be lifted out (or ripped out, if necessary, though this is undesirable), while the bottle can be thawed out by pouring some warm water into it in the morning. Other floating objects can be used to similar effect, provided they have a certain amount of 'give'. This has an added advantage in concrete and block ponds where the compressibility of such floating objects will relieve some of the pressure otherwise exerted on the pond walls themselves.

Perched upon this plant is a chironomid midge. Midges are one of many pests that can cause problems for your plants. However, they will rarely cause any serious problems to your fish. If you plan to spray your pond plants with any pesticide, remember that pesticides often contain chemicals that can prove lethal to your stock.

Once a hole has been created, it is possible to drain a small amount of water from underneath the ice to create a large air/water zone. But this will only work if the ice is strong enough not to collapse. At all costs, avoid creating a hole by striking the ice with a hammer or other heavy object. If you have ever done any diving and struck two stones together underwater, you will know only too well how loud and uncomfortable the sound and vibrations are. To inflict this on your fish would be unfair, cruel and potentially dangerous.

Winter is the season during which most life within the pond lies dormant. During the winter season, fish should not be fed and all less-than-hardy species of plants and animals should be removed for safe over-wintering.

12
Fish Health

As long as you adopt a reasonable approach to pondkeeping, fish are likely to enjoy good health most of the time. Minor ailments may develop occasionally, but many of these will quickly correct themselves of their own accord.

Without a doubt, prevention is incomparably better than cure, and the guidelines given in this book should go a long way towards achieving predominantly trouble-free conditions. Even so, outbreaks of disease will occur from time to time. Though most will be easy to rectify, some may prove very stubborn, or impossible, without professional assistance.

Fish are like any other pets in that they will leave us in no doubt when something is wrong. But it is up to us to interpret the symptoms correctly. Failure to do so can lead to suffering and even death.

It would be misleading to say that anyone can become an expert in the field of fish diseases simply by reading a section on the subject, such as this. Fish pathology is a complicated subject so, if in doubt, consult a professional, i.e. your local vet. There are many fish disease books on the market, too.

Some easily diagnosed diseases can now be treated effectively and quickly with proprietary brands of aquatic remedies. Others can only be treated with antibiotics which in many countries are only available on prescription. Most of these diseases are outlined below. The details should not, of course, be regarded as all-embracing or as providing a foolproof formula for success.

The three photos to the right depict three causes of health problems in ponds: (a) rotting organic material; (b) run-off water entering the pond; and (c) bird droppings.

DISEASE CHART

ICH OR WHITE SPOT

Symptoms	Body and fins covered in small white spots; in severe infestations, the spots may appear to join up; fins carried close to the body; violent shimmying; scratching against stones, plants and tank equipment
Disease	White Spot (Ichthyophthiriasis, or Ich.)
Causative Agent	*Ichthyophthirius multifiliis.*
Some Treatments	Numerous proprietary remedies are available, many based on Malachite Green, Methylene Blue or Copper Sulphate. Repeat treatment is often necessary to attack free-swimming stages of the parasite.

WHIRLING DISEASE

Symptoms	Darkened pigmentation in caudal region; whirling movements; progressive deformity of the backbone; survivors often exhibit (in addition) deformity of the gill covers, mandibles or skull.
Disease	Whirling Disease.
Causative Agent	*Myxosoma cerebralis.*
Some Treatments	No treatment is available; affected fish should be destroyed and pond disinfected.

FUNGUS

Symptoms	White or cream-colored fluffy patches on fins and/or body.
Disease	Cottonwool Disease or Fungus
Causative Agent	*Saprolegnia* and *Achyla* species.
Some Treatments	Proprietary remedies widely available—usually based on Phenoxethol, Malachite Green, Copper Sulphate, Potassium Permanganate or Methylene Blue. Salt Bath: 2-5 per cent solution for 10-15 minutes.

Ich (Ichthyophthiriasis) or white spot disease.

A fish infected with whirling disease—caused by Myxosoma cerebralis.

Goldfish suffering from a fungal disease caused by Saprolegnia sp.

CARP POX

Symptoms
Hard, whitish or cream-colored, waxy-like patches which may merge to cover substantial areas of the body.

Disease
Carp Pox.

Causative Agent
A virus.

Some Treatments
No treatment available but disease not normally fatal and often disappears spontaneously under good environmental conditions.

Carp pox: Hard, whitish or cream-colored patches.

Columnaris: Ulcers; shreading of fin rays.

COLUMNARIS

Symptoms
Localized or more general attack on body or fins leading to ulcers or shredding of fin rays. Blood streaks in fin rays usually develop.

Disease
Fin, Tail or Body Rot (Columnaris Disease.)

Causative Agent
Flexibacter columnaris and (possibly) other bacteria.

Some Treatments
Phenoxethol, Methylene Blue, Acriflavine, Chloramphenicol and other antibiotics. Some proprietary remedies available.

Whitish growths indicating fungus infection.

MOUTH FUNGUS

Symptoms
Whitish growths around the mouth gradually progressing into the jaw bones and anterior cheek area resulting in actual erosion of tissues.

Disease
Mouth Fungus (name is misleading because the causative agent is not a fungus.)

Causative Agent
Flexibacter columnaris and (possibly) other bacteria.

Some Treatments
As for Fin Rot.

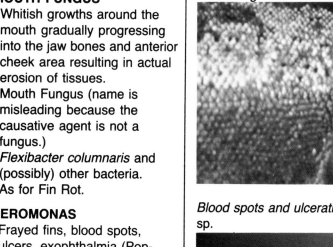

Blood spots and ulcerations caused by Aeromonas sp.

AEROMONAS

Symptoms
Frayed fins, blood spots, ulcers, exophthalmia (Pop-eye), individually or in combination.

Disease
Bacteremia (milder form.)
Septicemia (more acute form.)

Causative Agent
Aeromonas hydrophila.

Some Treatments
Chloramphenicol, Tetracyline, Oxolinic Acid (available in medicated flake form.) Some proprietary remedies available.

DROPSY

Symptoms Swollen abdomen and lifted scales, giving the body a 'pine-cone' appearance.

Disease Dropsy. (Bacterial hemorrhagic septicemia.)

Causative Agent *Aeromonas liquefaciens (ascitae* and/or *typica);* possibly others.

Some Treatments Usually no cure but Chloromycetin may help. Humane disposal of affected specimens, plus good hygiene, are the most effective methods of eradicating the disease and preventing its recurrence.

Fish showing signs of acute abdominal dropsy.

'OLD AGE' DISEASE

Symptoms No external signs of infection but gradual loss of color, appetite or condition.

Disease Non-specific bacterial infection.

Causative Agent One or more of the above or other species involved.

Some Treatments Phenoxethol, Acriflavine, Methylene Blue, Copper Sulphate, Malachite Green or low dose of a broad-spectrum antibiotic such as Chloramphenicol. Some proprietary remedies available.

A microscopic view of Dactylogyrus sp. *These gill parasites are the cause of many gill infections in pond fish. Luckily, however, there are some proven remedies available at your local pet store.*

GILL PARASITES

Symptoms Inflamed gills; excessive secretion of mucus on gills; accelerated respiration; gill covers may be held open; scratching of gill covers on plants, rocks and equipment.

Disease Gill Fluke infection.

Causative Agent *Dactylogyrus* spp.—a monogenetic trematode.

Some Treatments Some proprietary remedies are available based on a range of compounds, e.g., copper sulphate; salt bath (10-15 gm/liter) for 20 minutes or 25 gm/liter for 10-15 minutes; formalin (20 ml commercial formalin/100 liters) for 30-45 minutes; Methylene Blue (3 ml of 1 per cent stock solution/10 liters) indefinitely.

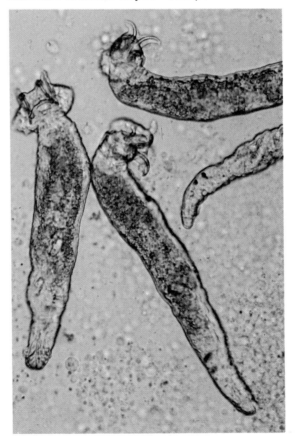

FISH LICE

Symptoms Nervous swimming and jumpiness; frequent vigorous scratching against rocks and equipment, often resulting in loss of scales; heavy infestations are accompanied by anemia and loss of color; the almost-transparent parasites can be seen attached to the body, mainly along the fin bases (adult parasites can be nearly 1 cm long.)

Disease Fish Louse Infection.

Causative Agent *Argulus* spp.—usually *A. foliaceus.*

Some Treatments Organophosphate bath (e.g. Dipterex or Naled. Follow instructions closely); potassium permanganate (1 gm/liter for 30-45 seconds or 1 gm/10 liters for 5-10 minutes); physical removal of individual parasites with forceps, followed by disinfection, e.g, an acriflavine-based compound.

TUBERCULOSIS

Symptoms Any one, or combination, of loss of color/condition, raised scales, exophthalmia, loss of appetite, emaciation, ulceration, frayed fins.

Disease Fish TB.

Causative Agent *Mycobacterium* spp.

Some Treatments No particularly effective treatment. Some antibiotics, e.g., Terramycin, may effect a cure when infection is not too severe.

FURUNCULOSIS

Symptoms Ulcers (often circular) in head region and/or body.

Disease Hole-in-the-head/body. (Ulcer Disease/Furunculosis.)

Causative Agent *Aeromonas salmonicida (A. hydrophila* may act as a secondary agent.)

Some Treatments Chloramphenicol, Tetracycline, Sulphonamides, e.g., Furan-based remedy.

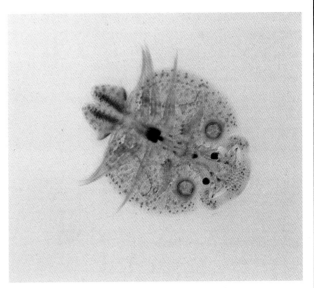

A microscopic view of the fish louse, Argulus sp.

This drawing shows the sympton of ulceration caused by tuberculosis.

This photo shows the most immediately obvious symptom of a Aeromonas *species infection—ulceration of the skin.*

ANCHOR WORM

Symptoms Long, thin, white, worm-like parasites (up to 20 cm in length) attached to the body and/or fins; two white egg-sacs at the posterior end are usually visible.

Disease Anchor Worm Infection.

Causative Agent *Lernaea* spp.

Some Treatments Some proprietary remedies are availabale, e.g., based on copper sulphate; potassium permanganate—as for *Argulus*. Salt bath (10-15 gm/liter for 20 minutes or 25 gm/liter for 10-15 minutes; Trichlorphon (1 mg/liter), indefinitely, may also dislodge the parasite.

SKIN DISEASE

Symptoms Inflamed patches on the skin and fins; erratic swimming; excessive secretion of body slime; accelerated respiration (if gills are affected); some loss of color; scratching on plants, rocks and equipment.

Disease Skin Fluke Infection (may also affect the gills.)

Causative Agent *Gyrodactylus* spp.—a monogenetic trematode.

Some Treatments As for *Dactylogyrus.*

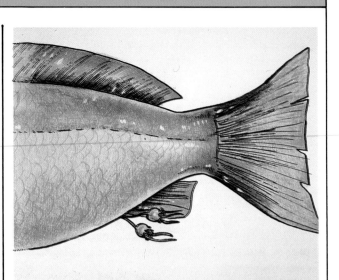

The appendages things attached to the underside of the fish are parasitic copepods of the genus Lernaea, popularly known as anchor worms.

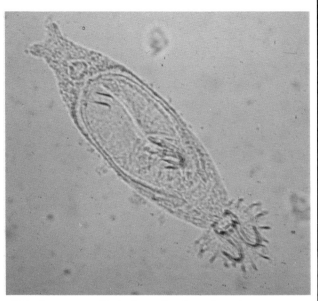

This is a magnified view of a Gyrodactylus *sp.*— monogenetic trematodes sometimes responsible for skin fluke infection.

CATS, HERONS, SNAILS AND AMPHIBIANS

Besides the pests mentioned in the section on Summer Maintenance, other pond visitors can present a problem. The two most common of these, at any time of year, are cats and herons.

It is extremely difficult to guarantee a pond that is both 100 per cent cat- and heron-proof and looks its best at all times. What we tend to do is compromise after an initial period of concerted effort at ridding ourselves of the problems.

Cats can be discouraged by persistence on the part of the pond-owner, who must be prepared to rush out and scare intruders away as often as necessary. After a time, either the frequency of the visits decreases, or the cats dash across the garden, ignoring the pond completely in their haste to avoid detection.

Paving slabs overlapping the pond edge, particularly if the level of the water is lowered by 6 in (15 cm) or more, can also help protect a pond against cats. So will dense clumps of marginal plants strategically placed around weak spots.

Herons do not normally alight directly in water, but land a short distance away and walk in. One of the most effective methods of controlling this visitor is to encircle the pond with a low fence about 6-8 in (15-20 cm) high, made out of sticks driven into the ground and linked together with fishing line. Some people take this further by stretching the line in a crisscross pattern across the pond itself. This ensures that all the shallow areas receive added protection. Netting is effective, but looks unsightly and is downright inconvenient.

Snails seem to be the center of some controversy among pond-owners. Some find them desirable, others will not tolerate them under any circumstances. The truth of the matter is that, if the population is kept under control by the other pond inhabitants or through baiting the adults and removing individuals or their jelly-like egg masses whenever they are spotted, then problems will hardly ever arise. I have always had snails in my ponds and have never found them troublesome.

Spring and summer visitors to a pond may include newts, frogs and toads. What you do about these depends to a large extent on your

Avoid these three potential problem spots: (A) cats can hide in surrounding brush; (B) crocodiles and snakes are a threat in areas where they exist; and (C) turtles can eat fish.

A photo of the gray heron, Ardea cinerea. *It resembles its cousin, the great blue heron, in more than appearance—both being predators. All herons are threats to garden pond fish.*

point of view. Newts will eat small fish if they catch them (cats and herons can take large ones), while adult male frogs and toads will attempt to embrace any passing object, fish included, in their short-sighted, but energetic efforts at spawning. While a few fish might be caught by ardent males from time to time, this is quite rare, particularly if there are not many frogs or toads and the pond offers good escape routes (such as deep water) for the fish.

If you wish or need to rid your pond of these amphibians, hand netting and removal to an alternative site is the only effective and humane method. I personally like having newts, frogs and toads in my ponds and so make no attempt to remove them.

This brightly colored snail is Helisoma nigricans. *Snails eat plants.*

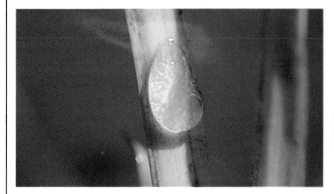

A common sight—egg clusters of the common pond snail. You may not see the snail itself. The eggs are the tell-tail sign.

Amphibians may be a welcome addition to many ponds, as many pond owners find these creatures fascinating.

bufo) *mating.*

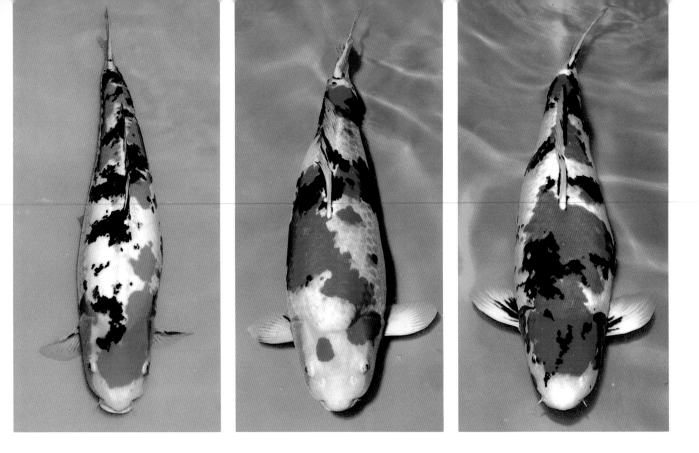

If you choose to have a koi pond, you will not be alone. Koi are growing in popularity around the globe. Koi come in many color varieties. Shown here are just a few winners of the 1988 All-Japan Koi Competition.

13

Selection of Fish For the Pond

Some types of fish, such as Koi and the Common Goldfish, can be recommended without reservation as being suitable for most water schemes (except wildlife ponds, unless they are 'wild-colored'.) Others, such as Orandas and Moors, are more delicate and cannot be recommended for areas which experience very harsh weather conditions. Yet others, e.g., Roach and Green Tench, can look and be out of place in any pond other than a wildlife one.

If you take into account personal likes and dislikes, opinions, local availability and other equally important factors, it soon becomes obvious that there is no single, magical set of rules that covers all possible permutations. But there are some general guidelines which might be found useful.

For a start, the more colorful, elaborate, large and 'aristocratic' types of fish are probably best displayed in formal ponds. Koi would therefore be a good choice for such a pond, assuming that it is large enough and deep enough to accommodate them.

Native species are best reserved for wildlife ponds. Do not forget, though, that wildlife ponds should also contain newts, frogs and toads. Including too many fish will virtually do away with this, since tadpoles will not survive long in a fully stocked pond of any type. Some wild species have long been available in a number of cultivated forms and these should not be included in wildlife ponds. Perhaps the best setting for these cultivated varieties is an informal pond. Golden Orfe, Golden Tench and Golden Rudd are the best known man-made varieties that fall into this category.

All fishes popularly known as goldfish, regardless of how fancy or of what color variety, are of the species Carassius auratus. *Goldfish are one of many species of fish that are suitable for inclusion into the garden pond.*

The above is a photo of one of the many varieties of goldfish, Carassius auratus. *This variety (the black moor) has protruding eyes and a dark coloration. It is popular in both the fish tank and the garden pond. Pet shops carry a wide selection of goldfish varieties.*

GOLDFISH *(Carassius auratus auratus)*

The full scientific name is given above to distinguish the Goldfish from its closest relative, the Gibel or Prussian Carp (*Carassius auratus gibelius.*) In practice, the two types overlap geographically and have interbred in the wild following intentional and unintentional introductions of wild and cultivated Goldfish into natural waters. Distinctions have consequently become blurred, with the shortened form of the name, i.e., *Carassius auratus* being used almost universally.

Some estimates put the number of varieties of Goldfish currently available at over 100. Relatively few of them have achieved widespread popularity, and of those that have, even fewer can be regarded as suitable for ponds. The best varieties are those with long slender bodies and/or relatively short fins. Most long-finned and overly elaborate varieties should be reserved for aquaria.

Types of Goldfish suitable for most ponds include Common Goldfish, London Shubunkins, Bristol Shubunkins, Comets and Fantails. Other more delicate types which can be kept with varying degrees of success (depending on factors such as climate) include Veiltails, Moors and Orandas (Calico, Red Cap and Metallic, i.e. single-colored.)

CRUCIAN CARP *(Carassius carassius)*

This species is very similar to the Goldfish but has a deeper body, a relatively small head and a convex outline to the dorsal fin. Crucian Carp do not change color as Goldfish do and are best suited to the wildlife pond community. Although the maximum stated size for this species is around 20 in (50 cm), pond specimens are generally smaller.

The above is Carassius carassius, *a close relative of the common goldfish* Carassius auratus. *While it is rarely seen in the pet trade,* Carassius carassius *is highly suitable for the garden pond, especially the wildlife-type. It can grow to around 20 inches (50 cm).*

CARP AND KOI *(Cyprinus carpio)*

Cyprinus carpio exists in a wide variety of forms, ranging from the drab-colored Carp to the colorful, slim-bodied, elegant Koi. Within the last decade, Koi-keeping has enjoyed a massive upsurge in popularity, largely as a result of ambitious commercial breeding programs established in many parts of the world not previously renowned for this. Japan continues to excel, but other countries, such as the UK, USA and Israel, have all made major inroads into the industry. The result is that, while the very best Koi still command high prices (and are likely to continue doing so), large numbers of inexpensive, colorful, non-pedigree Koi are now widely available.

If you are contemplating specializing in Koi, the best advice is to join a specialist society (most countries have at least one such society) and construct a pond specifically for Koi. If, on the other hand, you wish to include some Koi in your mixed pond selection, you will find something to meet your needs if you visit any reputable water garden center or aquatic shop. Fully-scaled specimens are generally hardier than partly-scaled or 'naked' ones. But do bear in mind that Koi grow large—2 ft (60 cm) and more is not uncommon. They are bred in 13 basic color groups.

TENCH *(Tinca tinca)*

Two varieties of this species are available; the Green or wild type, and a man-made, golden form. Both are quite popular with pond-owners. This fish is often sold as a scavenger—a label that should be regarded with suspicion. Tench will eat a wide range of foods, but not just carrion or left-overs as the scavenging tag would suggest. Being predominantly bottom feeders, these attractive fish tend to stir up debris and can therefore generate murky water conditions. Maximum lengths of around 28 in (70 cm) have been recorded, but most pond specimens grow to less than half this size.

Fish of the species Tinca tinca, *also known as tench, are predominantly bottom feeders and are great for the pond that has a sand bottom.*

Above and below: Tinca tinca, *the tench, is an attractive fish; yet, because it is a bottom feeder, it tends to create murky water conditions if the pond bottom is of soil. Tench grow to about 14 inches in the pond—up to about 28 inches in the wild.*

The golden orfe, Leuciscus idus, *is a colorful shoaler always on the move. They require a water supply rich in oxygen and are quite sensitive to some chemical water treatments.*

GOLDEN ORFE *(Leuciscus idus)*

The Golden Orfe is a man-made variety of the Ide, a slender-bodied, fast-swimming predatory species. Orfe are generally sold as 2-4 in (5-10 cm) specimens but the Ide can grow up to 3 ft (1 meter) in the wild. In captivity, however, most specimens do not tend to exceed 18 in (45 cm.) Orfe are colorful shoalers always on the move and require a rich oxygen supply. They are also quite sensitive to some treatments, e.g. organophosphates. So never exceed recommended dosages.

RUDD *(Scardinus erythrophthalmus)*

Considerable confusion often exists, particularly among newcomers to pondkeeping, concerning the correct identification of this species because of its superficial resemblance to the Roach (*Rutilus rutilus*.) Some of the main distinguishing characteristics are outlined in the accompanying table.

Besides the listed characteristics, Rudd are available as a golden, man-made variety as well as the wild-type, and tend to swim near the surface more frequently than Roach.

Species	Color of Fins	Origin of Pelvic Fins	Mouth
RUDD	All fins are reddish, but pelvics and anal are scarlet	Well in front of dorsal fin	Directed upward
ROACH	Upper part of caudal fin and whole of dorsal fin are dark; pelvics and anal—orange to red; pectorals and most of caudal—reddish	Almost in line with dorsal fin	Directed forward

OTHER SPECIES

Quite a few other coldwater species are now available, most of them better suited to wildlife schemes than ornamental ones.

Perch (*Perca fluviatilis*) and Pike (*Esox lucius*) are out-and-out predators and should be treated with caution. Bream (*Abramis brama*) are large—up to 30 in (80 cm) and tend to feed off the bottom of a pond, raising clouds of debris in the process. Bleak (*Alburnus albidus*), at around 6 in (15 cm), and Minnows (*Phoxinus phoxinus*) at around 4-5 in (12 cm), form large shoals. Dace (*Leuciscus leuciscus*) can grow up to 12 in (30 cm) and form mid-water shoals, while Chub (*Leuciscus cephalus*) grow much larger, i.e. 24 in (60 cm.) Mature specimens can even take frogs and other vertebrates.

Gudgeon (*Gobio gobio*), despite their bottom-dwelling reputation, can often be seen in mid-water. But this species maximum size about 8 in (20 cm) is quite sensitive to pollution and requires richly-oxygenated water.

Predatory Catfish, such as the Wels (*Siluris glanis*) which can grow to 9 ft (3 meters) and the American Channel/Blue Cats (*Ictalurus punctatus*) at around 3 ft (1 meter), must be considered unsuitable. The American Black Bullhead, *Ictalurus* (*Ameiurus*) *melas*, 12 in (30 cm) falls in the same category.

On the other hand, the Three-spined Stickleback (*Gasterosteus aculeatus*), maximum size 4 in (10 cm) and the Nine-spined Stickleback (*Pungitius pungitius*), maximum size around 3 in (7 cm), form interesting pond inhabitants, despite the former's reputation for carrying parasites. The Bitterling (*Rhodeus amarus*), often referred to as *R. sericeus* as well —4 in (9 cm)-is a fascinating species but requires the presence of freshwater mussels for successful spawning.

Two recent additions to the ever-expanding list are the Opaline/Moderlieschen (*Leucaspius delineatus*), measuring about 5 in (12 cm), and the similar sized American Fathead Minnow (*Pimephales promelas*) which is almost exclusively available in the golden form.

Various Sunfishes (all predatory to a greater or lesser extent), including Pumpkinseeds (*Lepomis gibbossus*), maximum length 10 in (25 cm), but nearly always smaller, and Rock Bass (*Ambloplites rupestris*) 12 in (30 cm) are also kept in ponds from time to time.

Some non-native wild species are deemed restricted and they should not be introduced into ponds for fear of major ecological disruption should they escape into native waters. Species such as the Grass Carp (*Ctenopharyngodon idella*) up to 4 ft (1.25 meters), the Silver Carp (*Hypophthalmichthys molitrix*) around 3 ft (1 meter) and the Zander (*Stizostedion lucioperca*) 4 ft (1.25 meters), fall into this category.

Gudgeon (Gobio gobio) *reaches a size of only about eight inches (20 cm). It is quite sensitive to water pollution and requires a water supply rich in oxygen.*

Leucaspius delineatus.   Phoxinus phoxinus.

Scardineus erythrophthalmus.   Rhodeus sericeus.

Rutilus rutilus.   Chondrostoma nasus.

Ctenopharyngodon idella.   Leuciscus idus.

Above: *This fish is an out-and-out predator and should be treated with caution. The perch* (Perca fluviatilis) *is suitable only for the wildlife pond and even then must be treated with caution. Unless you understand the behavior of this species, and know that your pond is a suitable habitat for both this fish and any other fish that are to live together in the pond, do not include the perch in your garden pond.*

14

Selection of Plants for the Pond

So many pond plants are available today that it is quite impossible even to mention every species or variety in a book such as this. Water Lilies alone come in a bewildering array of colors and sizes and deserve a book dedicated to them alone to do them full justice. It is hardly surprising, therefore, that I can only present a selection of plants in the following pages. A visit to any water garden center will serve to widen one's view and choice further and should be considered as a necessary follow-up to the selection of plants presented here.

SUBMERGED/OXYGENATING PLANTS

Although the available choice of these plants is quite restricted, oxygenators should be considered essential components of most ponds.

The best-known species is Canadian Pondweed or Anacharis (*Elodea canadensis*), but it does not appear to be as widely available as it once was. Far more common nowadays is the plant usually referred to as Crispa, or *Elodea crispa,* but more correctly known scientifically as *Lagarosiphon major.* Very similar in appearance is the plant commonly referred to as Densa (*Egeria densa*), the Argentinian Waterweed.

These three species can prove difficult to separate from each other. However, *E. densa* has larger, 1 in (2.5 cm), and lighter-colored leaves than *E. canadensis,* ½ in (1 cm), while *major* is more robust than either and has its leaves curled backwards.

There are many species of plants suitable for the garden pond. Fortunately, or perhaps unfortunately for some, your choice of pond plants will be limited by your local weather conditions and the type, size and depth of your pond.

Water lilies are a very popular pond plant. They are considered surface plants. They come in a wide range of available color varieties.

Duckweed is a floating plant. It can be seen to cover the entire surface of some ponds. To some it is attractive, while to others it is a pest. Ducks eat these plants.

Other popular oxygenators include various species of *Myriophyllum* particularly Parrot's Feather, variously known scientifically as *M. brasiliense, M. aquaticum* or *M. proserpinacoides,* and Spiked Water Milfoil (*M. spicatum.*) The former has submerged and aerial leaves, while the latter's foliage is predominantly submerged (though it produces aerial flowers.)

Hornwort (*Ceratophyllum demersum*) forms dense clumps of interweaving stems and fine leaves without ever producing roots. Curly Pondweed (*Potamogeton crispus*) looks almost like a crinkly brown seaweed. It is an attractive plant which produces insignificant aerial flowers.

Further examples of submerged oxygenating plants are Willow Moss (*Fontinalis antipyretica*), Water Violet (*Hottonia palustris*) Water Crowfoot (*Ranunculus aquatilis*), Starwort (*Callitriche verna*), Hair Grass (*Eleocharis acicularis*) which can also grow in moist soil, and even Tape Grass (*Vallisneria spiralis*), better known as an aquarium plant, and not particularly successful as a pond plant where weather is severe.

Myriophyllum brasiliense, *commonly known as parrot's feather, is a very attractive submerged plant having feather-like leaves.*

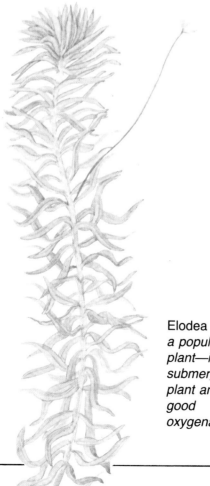

Elodea densa *is a popular pond plant—it is a submerged plant and a good oxygenator.*

161

A balance must always be maintained between fish and plants. Floating plants are attractive, but they can obscure the view of the fish.

Your edging can be attractively planted with a variety of plants. Care must be taken, however, to prevent excessive leaves and petals from falling into the pond and polluting the water.

FLOATING PLANTS

Floating plants can add color and shade to a pond. Small species include the various Duckweeds (*Lemna* spp) which are hardly ever sold intentionally, but often arrive as unintended introductions with other plants.

Fairy Moss (*Azolla caroliniana*) is, in reality, a fern and produces fluffy bright green mats on the water surface, turning reddish as autumn approaches.

Frogbit (*Hydrocharis morsus ranae*) is almost like a mini-Water Lily with white flowers, while the Water Soldier (*Stratiotes aloides*) looks almost like the top of a pineapple or a cactus. It sinks down to the bottom of the pond after flowering and rises to the surface again the following spring.

Some tropical and South European floating plants are also commonly available during the pond season but can only be regarded as summer additions. The best-known of these are Water Hyacinth (*Eichhornia crassipes*) and Water Chestnut (*Trapa natans* and *T. bicornis.*)

Two of the plants mentioned above, Duckweed and Fairy Moss, can sometimes undergo a population explosion, causing excessive surface cover and proving very difficult to eradicate.

Stratiotes aloides *is a beautiful flowering plant worthy of consideration for any suitable pond.*

Potamogeton natans *is a species of plant well suited for the wildlife pond. Commonly known as the broad-leafed pondweed, it is a surface plant that tends to spread.*

163

Everyone's tastes differ. Some people prefer many plants with few fish or amphibians; others like only fish in their pond. Even in regards to the degree of concentration of plants or animals in the pond, people's tastes vary. Depending on your own taste and desire, your pond can be highly concentrated with plants (as in the above photo), it can be devoid of all plants, or it can be anywhere in between.

SURFACE PLANTS

This group includes the most famous aquatic plants of all, the Water Lilies. For convenience, these will be dealt with separately below. Here, first, is a selection of other surface plants, which are distinguished from floating plants in that the latter's roots are suspended in midwater. Surface plants, on the other hand, have anchored roots.

Water Hawthorn (*Aponogeton distachyus*) is a South African plant which does well in European ponds. It has attractive oblong surface leaves and deliciously scented white flowers. The Water Fringe (*Nymphoides peltata*) is also extremely attractive and produces 'chains' of small lily-like leaves with yellow aerial flowers. The Brandy Bottle (*Nuphar luteum*) is a big, robust plant closely resembling a cultivated Lily and only really suitable for large ponds.

A better choice for other ponds would be the Golden Club (*Orontium aquaticum*) with its unusual blue-green leaves. This plant is also unusual in that its leaves can project upward from the surface of the pond if the water is very shallow, creating the impression that it is a marginal rather than a surface plant.

For the wildlife pond, the Broad-leaved Pondweed (*Potamogeton natans*), though spreading in habit, and the Amphibious Bistort (*Polygonum amphibium*), with its delicate pink flower spikes, could be considered useful additions.

The most famous of all aquatic plants is the water lily. Water lilies are surface plants suitable for most garden ponds.

Luronium natans (frog cabbage), as can be seen in this photo, often lives up to its name of being a surface plant that spreads. It is a profuse grower that may well require some weeding to keep it under control.

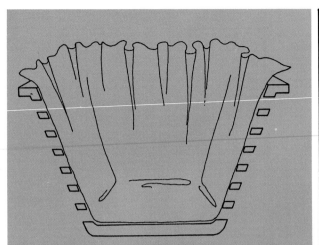

Planting containers can be purchased at your local pet shop, or made by hand by placing a piece of excess liner or other suitable material in a suitable basket . . .

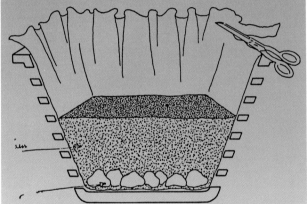

Place a few stones in the bottom of the container to add weight; fill to about half-way with a suitable planting medium; and trim the excess liner . . .

Your planting basket will provide your pond plants with a place to take root and grow. It will also prevent excessive root spread and and allow for easy removal of the plant and maintenance of the pond.

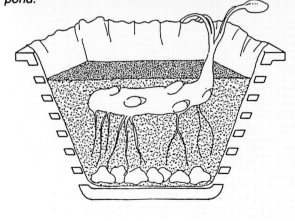

WATER LILIES

These magnificent plants have been cultivated and developed for so long, and to such an extent, that we now have a situation not dissimilar to that surrounding roses. Every year, new varieties seem to appear, adding extra excitement to an already exciting scene.

Lilies are generally classified as either tropical or hardy. Unless one lives in the tropics or subtropics, the former can only be regarded as suitable for indoor ponds (or outdoor ones for a brief period at the height of summer.) Hardy Lilies, as their name suggests, do not suffer from this restriction. There are Lilies to meet every need, from the smallest decorative tubs to the largest ponds.

To make sense of a potentially confusing state of affairs, growers use one or the other method of grouping, usually based on recommended planting depths for individual varieties, their relative rates of growth, or their eventual maximum size. Purchase lilies from your local petshop so they will be more suitable for your climate.

A lovely shot of a beautiful tropical water lily with a most attractive hue.

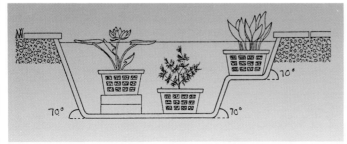

The lilies in the photo above were planted in baskets as shown in the drawing to the left. Planting-baskets are inconspicuous to the eye and will neither damage nor endanger the plant.

MARGINAL PLANTS

The range of these 'transition zone' plants that grow with water on the one side and dry land on the other, expands with every passing season. Irises, in particular, are now available in a host of shapes, colors and sizes, mirroring (though not to quite the same extent) the sort of attention afforded to Water Lilies. Here is a selection of what you can expect to find:

Marginal plants serve mostly an esthetic purpose. The very attractive marginal above is one of the many Iris *varieties*.

Iris pseudacorus *is another very attractive marginal that can enhance the setting of your pond.*

Type	Color of Blooms	Water Depth	Approx. Overall Height
Iris kaempferi varieties	White, pink, lavender, blue	Moist soil or roots barely covered	Up to 36 in (90 cm)
I. laevigata varieties	White or blue	2-4 in (5-10 cm)	30 in (75 cm)
I. laevigata Rose Queen*	Pink	2-4 in (5-10 cm)	30 in (75 cm)
I. laevigata variegata	Lavender-blue (Variegated leaves)	2-4 in (5-10 cm)	30 in (75 cm)
I. pseudoacorus Yellow Flag)	Yellow	Up to 18 in (45 cm)	Up to 60 in (150 cm)
I. pseudocorus variegatus	Yellow (Variegated leaves)	Up to 18 in (45 cm)	Up to 60 in (150 cm)

*This variety is probably a hybrid between Iris laevigata *and* I. kaempferi.

Though some marginal plants can stand being planted quite deeply, most prefer only shallow water, while a few only do well in moist soil. If planting containers are used, it may be a good idea to place these close to the maximum recommended planting depths for tall species. This will prevent the clumps toppling over in windy conditions.

Irises all do well as border plants. They are good bloomers, producing very attractive flowers. One of the wonderful qualities of irises is the wide range of available color varieties in which they can be acquired and cultivated. They can be cut and serve as table decorations, too.

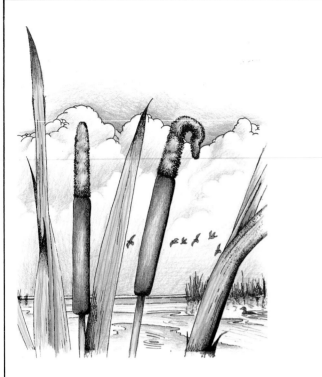

An artists drawing of Typha minima, *a suitable marginal. Below is a photo of* Caltha palustris *a very attractive flowering marginal.*

ALPHABETICAL LIST OF SELECTED MARGINAL PLANTS

Acorus (Sweet Flag)—Narrow, pointed strap-like leaves. Three types are usually available: *A. calamus*, 30 in (up to 75 cm) tall; *A. gramineus* and *A. gramineus variegatus* both 8-12 in (20-30 cm.) Planting depth: moist soil, down to 2 in (5 cm) of water.

Alisma (Water Plantain)—Two species are usually available; *A. lanceolatum* and *A. plantago aquatica* (Great Water Plantain.) Lanceolate green leaves with whitish/pinkish flower spikes up to 12 in (30 cm) tall. Planting depth: moist soil or shallow water.

Butomus umbellatus (Flowering Rush)—Long, narrow leaves with small pink or purple, red-centered flowers. Can grow to 48 in (120 cm.) Planting depth: down to 6 in (15 cm) or deeper.

Calla palustris (Bog Arum)—Shiny green, heart-shaped leaves with white 'flowers' (actually a spathe or modified leaf) encircling yellow rod-like, true flowers. Grows to around 8 in (20 cm.) Planting depth: moist soil or shallow water.

Caltha palustris (Marsh Marigold or King Cup)—Yellow early flowering marginal also available as a double form, *C. p. plena.* A white variety, *C. p. alba,* can grow to 36 in (90 cm), but the others are smaller. Planting depth: moist soil or shallow water.

Carex (Sedge)—Several species and varieties of this grass-like plant are available. Most will spread very quickly. Average height about 12 in (30 cm.) Planting depth: moist soil or shallow water.

Cyperus (Umbrella Grass)—Graceful, sedge-like plants, *C. longus,* can grow up to 48 in (120 cm), *C. eragrostis* up to 24 in (60 cm.) Planting depth: down to 6 in (15 cm.)

Eriophorum (Cotton Grass)—Grassy leaves with elegant white cotton-like seedheads. Several species are available, 12-18 in (30-45 cm) tall. Planting depth: moist soil or shallow water.

Glyceria aquatica variegata (Manna Grass)—Attractive, variegated grassy leaves. Can grow up to 36 in (90 cm.) Planting depth: moist soil or shallow water.

Houttuynia cordata—Heart-shaped leaves, red stems and white flowers. Can grow up to 18 in (45 cm.) A double form, *H. c. plena,* is also available. Planting depth: moist soil or shallow water.

Juncus (Rush)—A few species up to 18 in (45 cm) are available for pond use. Grass-like leaves with roundish brown/black flower heads. Planting depth: moist soil or shallow water.

Lobelia cardinalis (Lobelia)—Elegant plant with reddish leaves and stems and brilliant red flowers. Can grow up to 48 in (120 cm) and may need some protection in winter. Planting depth: moist soil, down to 6 in (15 cm) of water.

Lysichitum (Lysichiton or Skunk Cabbage)—The latter name more correctly applies to *Symplocarpus foetidus*) *L. americanum* has large yellow arum–like smelly flowers, 12 in (up to 30 cm) which precede the leaves. The foliage can grow up to 48 in (120 cm.) *L. camtschatcense* is similar in size, but has white flowers that do not smell. Only suitable for large ponds. Planting depth: moist soil or shallow water.

Mentha aquatica (Water Mint)—Similar to the garden equivalent and just as invasive. Flowers are light blue, borne on stems up to 36 in (90 cm) high. Planting depth: moist soil or shallow water.

Menyanthes trifoliata (Bog or Buck Bean)—Light green leaves, pinkish flowers. Grows only to around 9 in (24 cm) high. Planting depth: moist soil or shallow water.

Mimulus (Monkey Flower)—Various types available with yellow, orange, red-spotted and blue flowers. Some can grow to 36 in (90 cm), but most remain smaller. Planting depth: down to 4 in (10 cm.)

Myosotis palustris (Water Forget-me-not)—Small leaves, small light blue flowers. Grows to around 9 in (24 cm.) Planting depth: moist soil or shallow water.

Pontederia cordata (Pickerel Weed)—Shiny green, roughly heart-shaped leaves. Blue flower spikes. Can grow to 24 in (60 cm.) Planting depth: prefers shallow water but can be grown successfully in water even as deep as 12 in (30 cm.)

Ranunculus lingua grandiflora (Spearwort)— Potentially invasive plant with yellow flowers borne on stems 36 in (90 cm) high. Planting depth: shallow water.

Sagittaria (Arrowhead)—Various types are available. All have arrowshaped leaves and white flower spikes (double in *S. japonica* 'Flore Pleno'.) Planting depth: preferably down to around 6 in (15 cm), but will grow in deeper water.

Scirpus (including Zebra Rush or Porcupine Quill)—*S. albescens* is variegated. *S. tabernaemontanii zebrinus* has white/cream bands. Both are potentially invasive and can grow to around 48 in (120 cm) or taller. Planting depth: down to around 6 in (15 cm.)

Typha (Reedmace)—Three species (all invasive) are often available: *T. latifolia* (8 ft) 2.4 m, *T. angustifolia* (up to 6 ft) 1.8 m and the best for most ponds, *T. minima* (18 in) 45 cm. Planting depth: down to around 6 in (15 cm) for *T. minima,* deeper for the others.

Zantedeschia aethiopica (Arum Lily)—Glossy green arrow/spear-shaped leaves. Impressive 'flowers' (actually a spathe or modified leaf), with elegant, yellow rod-like column (spadix) of true flowers inside. Can grow to 36 in (90 cm.) Planting depth: down to 12 in (30 cm.)

Many plants suitable for your pond can be purchased at a fraction of the cost if they are purchased when small and allowed time to mature in your own pond or aquarium. Such plants should be potted to allow them to root easily.

SUGGESTED READING

The following books, all published by T.F.H. Publications, Inc. and all available at pet shops everywhere, are recommended for use by anyone interested in obtaining more information about garden ponds and their inhabitants.

GOLDFISH: A Complete Introduction
By Robert Mertlich
Hardcvr. CO-019 ISBN 0-86622-268-5
Softcvr. CO-019S ISBN 0-86622-350-9
Audience: This book, authored by America's leading goldfish authority, provides for the first time many secrets of successful goldfish breeders. The information in this book is basically for beginners trying their hand with fancy, as well as common, goldfish. But it is much more than that, as author Mertlich shares his secrets in keeping goldfish happy and healthy through every possible situation you might encounter, whether in the home aquarium, the garden pool or a wading pool.
5½ x 8½, 128 pages. Completely illustrated with over 100 full-color photos.

KOI VARIETIES: Japanese Colored Carp-Nishikigoi
By Dr. Herbert R. Axelrod
TFH PS-875 ISBN 0-86622-885-3
Contents: What are Nishikigoi? How Koi Became Popular. Thirteen Basic Varieties. Real and Artificial Coloring in Koi. Doitsu, The German Carp. Keeping Koi. Long-finned and Pygmy Koi. Catalog of Prize Winning Fish.
This Colorful book covers the many varieties available, selection, and history of the increasingly popular koi. For the avid breeder or pond owner who wants specialized information about these prized fish. Contains a revealing section about the genetics of Koi.
Hard cover, 8½ x 11", 144 pages. Over 250 full-color photos.

GOLDFISH AND KOI IN YOUR HOME
By Dr. Herbert R. Axelrod and William Vorderwinkler
TFH H-909 ISBN 0-86622-041-0
Contents: What Your Goldfish Need. Setting Up the Aquarium and Choosing the Plants. How to Choose Goldfish. Goldfish Varieties. How to Breed Goldfish. How to Raise Quality Goldfish. Goldfish Diseases. The Garden Pool.
Audience: For the home aquarium and tropical fish hobbyist. This book contains complete data on care and feeding, treatment of fish diseases, water conditions, and everything necessary for the home owner of goldfish and koi. Ages 13 and above.
Hard cover, 5½ x 8", 208 pages. 91 black and white photos, 125 color photos.

KOI AND GARDEN PONDS: A Complete Introduction
By Dr. Herbert R. Axelrod
Hardcvr. CO-040 ISBN 0-8622-398-3
Softcvr. CO-040S ISBN 0-8622-399-1
Audience: For anyone interested in the Japanese carp and for owners of garden pools. This is a truly beautiful book with great value as an identifier of the many different scale and color patterns of koi.
5½ x 8½, 96 pages. Contains 104 full-color photos and 108 full-color line drawings.

KOI OF THE WORLD—Japanese Colored Carp
By Dr. Herbert R. Axelrod
TFH H-947 ISBN 0-87666-092-8
Until the publication of *Koi Varieties,* this book was far and away the most up-to-date and colorful book about koi in the English language. Covering such important topics as the basic needs of koi, breeding koi, koi diseases, fish sales and koi shows, the book is loaded with excellent, big, full-color photos of different koi varieties, all properly identified. This is the first English-language text ever to capture the romance of koi and make it understandable to occidental eyes. Big and beautiful and definitely a great value.
Hard cover, 9 x 12", 240 pages. Contains 327 full-color photos, 27 black and white photos.

GOLDFISH GUIDE
By Dr. Yoshiichi Matsui
TFH PL-2011 ISBN 0-87666-545-8
Contents: Introduction. Goldfish History. Physically Speaking. Races or Varieties of Goldfish. Chinese Goldfish. The Environment. Goldfish Indoors. Food and Feeding. Diseases and Natural Enemies. Goldfish Genetics. Breeding. Garden Pools. Water Lilies. Goldfishkeeping in Great Britain. A Summary. Carp. The Care of Carp.
Audience: Anyone with an interest in goldfish—whether they're kept in the house or in a decorative outside pool or pond—will benefit greatly from this book. Written by a foremost Japanese fancier, it combines plenty of bedrock information about keeping and breeding with an in-depth discussion of the many shapes and color varieties.
Hard cover, 5½ x 8", 256 pages. Illustrated with 100 full-color photos.

GENETICS FOR THE AQUARIST
By Dr. J. Schroder
TFH PS-656 ISBN 0-87666-461-3
This is the only book in the English language that deals entirely with the genetics of fish kept as pets. Invaluable for an understanding of trait inheritance in fish.
Soft Cover, 5½ x 8", 125 pages. 10 black and white photos, 59 color photos, 30 line drawings, 12 tables.

KOI AND GARDEN PONDS: A Complete Introduction
By Dr. Herbert R. Axelrod
Hardcvr. CO-040 ISBN 0-86622-398-3
Softcvr. CO-040S ISBN 0-86622-399-1
For anyone interested in the Japanese carp and for owners of garden pools. This is a truly beautiful book with great value as an identifier of the many different scale and color patterns of koi.
5½ x 8½, 96 pages. Contains 104 full-color photos and 108 full-color line drawings.

GARDEN PONDS: A Complete Introduction
By Al David
Hardcvr. CO-017 ISBN 0-86622-266-9
Softcvr. CO-017S ISBN 0-86622-298-7
This highly colorful book shows and tells readers how to set up a garden pond or pool. Authoritative advice is given about making the pond, how to protect it against enemies, which fish and plants to put into it, and how to keep it beautiful.
5½ x 8½, 96 pages. Contains 114 full-color photos and 22 full-color line drawings.

WATER GARDENS FOR PLANTS AND FISH
By Charles B. Thomas
TFH TS-102 ISBN 0-866232-942-6
Highly illustrated with full-color photos, plus full-color diagrams and diagnostic drawings, this book has been written by one of the world's foremost commercial water gardeners. It concentrates on providing practical advice about setting up a garden pond and keeping it beautiful. Easy to read and highly useful.
Hardcover 5½ x 8, 192 pages. Over 200 full-color illustrations.

TEXTBOOK OF FISH HEALTH
By Dr. George W. Post
TFH H-1043 ISBN 0-87666-599-7
Owners of expensive fish like koi need a good understanding of how fish become ill, and this book is a complete account of all of the mechanisms and organisms that cause diseases in fishes, with emphasis on the diseases of bacterial and viral origin. Covers history, signs, treatment and distribution. Illustrated with hundreds of full-color photos that are excellent aids in the identification of diseases and their causes.
For scientists, hobbyists, fish culturists, students. College level.

Photo credits: Dr. Herbert R. Axelrod, Dr. Guido Dingerkus, Jaroslav Eliáš, Michael Gilroy, Burkhard Kahl, Charles O. Masters, F. Meyer, Midori Shobo, Hans Richter, Fred Rosenzweig, Taisho Sanshoku, Vince Serbin, Dr. B.F. Snieszko, Paul Stetson, Edward Taylor, D. Terver (Nancy Aquarium), Charles Thomas (Lilypons, Inc.), Dr. Arthur Topilow, H. Untergasser, Van Ness Water Gardens, Dr. Jörg Vierke, Vitakraftwerke, Uwe Werner, Lothar Wischnath, Yokoyama Printing Co. and R. Zukal.

Art by: Scott Boldt and John R. Quinn.

Index

Numbers in **Bold** refer to illustrations

Measurement Conversion Factors

When you know—	Multiply by—	To find—
Length:		
Millimeters (mm)	0.04	inches (in)
Centimeters (cm)	0.4	inches (in)
Meters (m)	3.3	feet (ft)
Meters (m)	1.1	yards (yd)
Kilometers (km)	0.6	miles (mi)
Inches (in)	2.54	centimeters (cm)
Feet (ft)	30	centimeters (cm)
Yards (yd)	0.9	meters (m)
Miles (mi)	1.6	kilometers (km)
Area:		
Square centimeters (cm^2)	0.16	square inches (sq in)
Square meters (m^2)	1.2	square yards (sq yd)
Square kilometers (km^2)	0.4	square miles (sq mi)
Hectares (ha)	2.5	acres
Square inches (sq in)	6.5	square centimeters (cm^2)
Square feet (sq ft)	0.09	square meters (m^2)
Square yards (sq yd)	0.8	square meters (m^2)
Square miles (sq mi)	1.2	square kilometers (km^2)
Acres	0.4	hectares (ha)
Mass (Weight):		
Grams (g)	0.035	ounces (oz)
Kilograms (kg)	2.2	pounds (lb)
Ounces (oz)	28	grams (g)
Pounds (lb)	0.45	kilograms (kg)
Volume:		
Milliliters (ml)	0.03	fluid ounces (fl oz)
Liters (L)	2.1	pints (pt)
Liters (L)	1.06	quarts (qt)
Liters (L)	0.26	U.S. gallons (gal)
Liters (L)	0.22	Imperial gallons (gal)
Cubic centimeters (cc)	16.387	cubic inches (cu in)
Cubic meters (cm^3)	35	cubic feet (cu ft)
Cubic meters (cm^3)	1.3	cubic yards (cu yd)
Teaspoons (tsp)	5	millimeters (ml)
Tablespoons (tbsp)	15	millimeters (ml)
Fluid ounces (fl oz)	30	millimeters (ml)
Cups (c)	0.24	liters (L)
Pints (pt)	0.47	liters (L)
Quarts (qt)	0.95	liters (L)
U.S. gallons (gal)	3.8	liters (L)
U.S. gallons (gal)	231	cubic inches (cu in)
Imperial gallons (gal)	4.5	liters (L)
Imperial gallons (gal)	277.42	cubic inches (cu in)
Cubic inches (cu in)	0.061	cubic centimeters (cc)
Cubic feet (cu ft)	0.028	cubic meters (m^3)
Cubic yards (cu yd)	0.76	cubic meters (m^3)
Temperature:		
Celsius (°C)	multiply by 1.8, add 32	Fahrenheit (°F)
Fahrenheit (°F)	subtract 32, multiply by 0.555	Celsius (°C)